SO-ASN-822

Dr. Neil T. Anderson

Released

FROM

BONDAGE

Publishers Since 1798

THOMAS NELSON PUBLISHERS
NASHVILLE

Copyright © 1993 by Neil T. Anderson.

All rights reserved. Written permission must be secured from the publisher to use or reproduce any part of this book, except for brief quotations in critical reviews or articles.

Published in Nashville, Tennessee, by Thomas Nelson, Inc.

Unless indicated otherwise, Scripture quotations are from *The New American Standard Bible*, © The Lockman Foundation 1960, 1962, 1963, 1968, 1971, 1972, 1975, 1977.
Scripture quotations designated NIV are from *The Holy Bible: New International Version*, © 1973, 1978, 1984 by the International Bible Society. Published by Zondervan Bible Publishers, Grand Rapids, Michigan.
Scripture quotations designated NKJV are from *The Holy Bible: New King James Version,* © 1982 by Thomas Nelson, Inc., Nashville, Tennessee.

Cover design by Garborg Design Works

Library of Congress Cataloging-in-Publication Data

Anderson, Neil T., 1942–
    Released from bondage / Neil T. Anderson.
        p.   cm.
    Originally published: San Bernardino, CA : Here's Life Publishers, 1991.
    ISBN 0-8407-4388-3 (pbk.)
    1. Spiritual warfare. 2. Pastoral Counseling 3. Suffering — Religious aspects — Christianity.   4. Anderson, Neil T., 1942–   . I. Title.
[BV4509.5.A53   1992]
248.8'6 — dc20

                                                    92-41366
                                                    CIP

Printed in the United States of America

3 4 5 6 7 8 9 — 96 95 94 93

I dedicate this book
to my dear friends, Ron and Carole Wormser,
and to the courageous people who have shared their stories.

May the Lord protect them and use their faithful service and
testimony to help many live a victorious life in Christ.
They have proven themselves to be disciples:
"By this is My Father glorified, that you bear much fruit,
and so prove to be My disciples" (John 15:8).

Acknowledgments

There are no "self-made" people. Only the "God-made" exist spiritually and bear fruit. The true children of God are born from above. They mature as their minds are renewed by the Word of God, and by overcoming the harsh realities of a fallen world. God does not save us from the trials and tribulations of this world, but from a Godless eternity. We enter into this eternal life the moment we put our trust in Him. He sets us free from our past and works through the difficulties of life to produce godly character.

This book is about finding our freedom in Christ and surviving in a world whose god is roaring around like a lion seeking someone to devour. Jesus said, "In Me you have peace. In the world you have tribulation, but take courage; I have overcome the world" (John 16:33).

I want to acknowledge the people from whom you will hear in this book. They have found their peace *in* Christ and have overcome the world. They have graciously allowed their stories to be told. In the process of working with us, it required them to relive the horror they went through. In my mind they are heroes of the faith. "They overcame him [Satan] because of the blood of the Lamb, and because of the word of their testimony" (Revelation 12:11). Their only motive for sharing their stories is to help others.

I also want to acknowledge my dear friends, Ron and Carole Wormser, who made this book possible. They are responsible for much of the writing and editing, and they personally counseled some of the people in this book. They are a precious couple who have served the Lord in missionary service for more than thirty years.

Contents

Introduction

Setting Captives Free

Where are the hurting?
What is their hope?

When I graduated from seminary, I was looking forward to being the captain of a Gospel Ship. We would sail off into the eternal sunset, rescuing people from the watery abyss. We would have Bible classes, clubs for the kiddies and sports for the athletically inclined (for the purpose of outreach, of course). Everybody would love one another.

Off I sailed on my first assignment and it wasn't long before I noticed a dark ship sailing alongside. On that ship were people with all kinds of problems. They were struggling with alcohol, sex, drugs and abuse of every conceivable kind. I suddenly realized that I was on the wrong ship. God had called me to be the captain of the dark ship. Through a series of life-transforming events, I ended up being that captain—and to my surprise I found out it was the same ship!

The needy are not only "out there" somewhere. Our churches are filled with hurting people wearing masks, frightened that someone may find out what's really going on inside of them. They would love nothing more than to have some hope, affirmation and help.

This book is about being released from that kind of bondage. You will read actual accounts of courageous people who have agreed to tell their stories from their perspective. They were already committed evangelical Christians before our encounter together. Some are in full-time ministry. Only their names, occupations and geographical references have been changed to protect their identity. I assure you that what they share is true and they in no way represent a few isolated cases.

We have hundreds of similar stories from personal counseling and thousands that could be shared from conferences. What's at stake isn't my reputation or transient ministry, but the integrity of the church and countless millions who are counting on the church to take its rightful place in God's kingdom program of setting captives free. I hope you will find great personal help in reading these pages, but beyond that, it is my earnest prayer that you will gain insights which will enable you to become a part of a captive-freeing movement of God which is beginning to grow in the church.

Hope for the Hopeless

One day I received a call from a colleague in the ministry. We chatted about what God was doing in our respective lives. After recounting testimonies of marriages saved and people freed from bondage, he shifted to the real intent of his call. "Neil," he began, "I recall you saying that a husband can get caught in a role conflict if he tries to counsel his own wife. I have had the privilege of helping others find freedom in Christ, but trying to help my own family is another matter. Could you possibly find time to see my wife, Mary? She is a wonderful lady, and people see her as composed, but she struggles inwardly on a daily basis."

Mind you, this is the wife of a man in ministry. But then, why wouldn't Satan attack those in the front lines of the battle?

I met twice with Mary. The first day we just got acquainted. The second day I walked her through the Steps to Freedom in Christ, which address seven main areas where Satan could have an opportunity to gain a stronghold in our lives. (These Steps to Freedom are in the appendix.) A week later I received this letter from Mary:

Dear Neil:
How can I say thanks? The Lord allowed me to spend

time with you just when I was concluding that there was no hope for me to ever break free from the downward spiral of continual defeat, depression and guilt. I did not know my place in Christ or recognize the enemy's accusations.

Everyone thought I was as put together on the inside as I was on the outside.

Having literally grown up in church and having been a pastor's wife for twenty-five years, everyone thought I was as put together on the inside as I was on the outside. On the contrary, I knew there was no infrastructure on the inside and often wondered when the weight of trying to hold myself together would cause my life to fall apart and come crumbling down. It seemed as if sheer determination was the only thing that kept me going.

When I left your office last Thursday it was a beautiful, crystal-clear day with snow visible on the mountains, and it felt like a film had been lifted from over my eyes. The tape player was playing a piano arrangement of *It Is Well With My Soul*. The words of the song fairly exploded in my mind with the realization that it was well in my soul . . . for the first time in years.

The next day at work my immediate response to "How are you today?" was "I'm doing great! How about you?" In the past I would have mumbled something about being almost alive. The next comment I heard was, "Boy, something must have happened to you yesterday."

I want to shout from the rooftops what has taken place in my life.

I have heard the same songs and read the same Bible verses as before, but it is as if it's all totally new. There is underlying joy and peace in the midst of the same circumstances that used to bring defeat and discouragement. For the first time, I have wanted to read my Bible and pray. It is hard to contain myself—I want to shout from the rooftops what has taken place in my life, but my real desire is for my life itself to do the shouting.

Already the deceiver has tried to plant thoughts in my mind that this won't last, that it's just another gimmick that won't work. The difference is that now I know those are lies from Satan and not the truth. What a difference freedom in Christ makes!

With gratitude,

Mary

What a difference indeed! Is there something special about Neil Anderson that made this counseling session so effective? Do I have some unique gift from God or special anointing? No, I don't think so. In fact, there are people all over the world using the same truths that I do to help people find their freedom in Christ, with similar results. So how does one explain such results?

What Is Mental Health?

Psychologists and mental health experts generally agree that people are mentally healthy if they are in touch with reality and relatively free of anxiety. From a secular view, then, every person in this book would be considered mentally ill, and so would anybody else under spiritual attack. Seen through the grid of our western culture, these people have either a neurological or psychological problem.

If someone hears voices or sees an apparition and the counselor doesn't, the secular counselor concludes that the person has lost touch with reality and he or she will be put on anti-psychotic medication to stop the voices. Yet I have counseled hundreds of people who are hearing voices, and to this day, every one has been demonic (or MPD). With the person's cooperation, it usually takes an average of two to three-and-a-half hours to free a Christian from that influence.

In 1 Timothy 4:1, we learn "that in later times some will abandon the faith and follow deceiving spirits and things taught by demons" (NIV). It is easier for me to believe that these people who hear voices are under spiritual attack than to believe they are mentally ill and that their mind has somehow split apart and carries on a dialogue with the other half. After hearing their stories, I have told hundreds that they are not going crazy, but that there is a spiritual battle going on for their minds. You can't imagine the relief that brings to troubled people.

If they are mentally deranged, I can't offer them a very positive prognosis. But if there is a battle going on for their minds, we can win that war. I do believe, however, that the mind can dissociate during severe trauma as a defensive means to mentally survive. I will discuss that phenomenon in the last chapter.

Satan Paralyzes His Prey

Anyone under spiritual attack would also fail on the second criterion for mental health—relative freedom from anxiety. Fear is a given for those caught in bondage. Like a lion, Satan's deceptive roar (1 Peter 5:8) paralyzes his prey in fear, but we are to remain firm in our faith (i.e., what we believe). Fear and faith are mutually exclusive. If fear of the unknown is governing one's life, then faith in God isn't. Only the fear of the Lord is compatible with biblical faith. In reality this lion named "Satan" has no teeth, but he is, outrageously, getting away with gumming Christians to death!

A pastor friend called asking for my help. His wife was faced with what appeared to be a terminal illness and he called me because she was experiencing tremendous fear. As we talked, she proclaimed in tears that she may not be a Christian. I was astonished. She was one of the most loving, pious examples of Christianity I had ever known. Yet here she was, facing the possibility of death without the assurance of salvation. I responded, "Sweetheart, if you're not a Christian, I'm in deep trouble. Why would you think that?" She replied, "Sometimes, when I go to church, I think these awful thoughts about God and dirty thoughts go through my mind." "That's not you," I assured her. Half an hour later she understood the origin of those thoughts and Satan's tactics; the thoughts were gone and so was her fear.

If those thoughts had been her thoughts, then what could she have concluded about her nature? "How can I be a Christian and have those kinds of thoughts?" she reasoned, and so do millions of other well-meaning Christians. Exposing the lie and understanding the battle for the mind is to win half the battle. The other half is having a true knowledge of God and knowing who you are as a child of God.

Where Mental Health Begins

I believe mental health begins with a true knowledge of God and who we are as His children. If you know that God loves you, will never leave you nor forsake you, and has prepared a place for you for all eternity . . . if you know that your sins are forgiven, that God will supply all your needs and enable you to live a responsible life in Christ . . . if you have no fear of death because eternal life is something you possess now and forever . . . if you know that . . . if you deeply know and believe that . . . would you be mentally healthy? Surely, you would!

If that true knowledge of God and who we are is where mental health begins, let me quickly add that the greatest determinant of mental illness is a distorted knowledge of God—a pathetic understanding of your relationship with Him and ignorance of who you are as a child of God. That is why secular counselors often hate religion. Most of their clients are very religious! Visit a "psych" ward and you will observe some of the most religious people you have ever seen, but they are not people who have a true understanding of who they are in Christ. Since the secular counselors are ignorant of the spiritual world, they wrongly blame pastors and churches for their clients' distress. (Although I must admit there are some pretty sick pastors and churches who do indeed create problems for people.)

The Gospel in Counseling

I pray for the day that Christian counseling can be identified on the basis of two definitive questions. First, *how does the gospel enter into the counseling procedure?* Are hurting people just a product of their past, or are they primarily a product of the work of Christ on the cross? Past experiences can and do have a profound effect on present day living and perspectives, but can we be free from our past—and how?

Various attempts are often made to fix the past. You can't fix the past; you cannot go back and undo what has been done. Much, much better is the truth that you can be a brand new creation in Christ and be set free from the past by establishing a new identity in Christ and forgiving those who offended you. The cross of Christ is the center of human history and experience; without that there is no gospel and there is no forgiveness. (This is the subject of my first book, *Victory Over the Darkness.*)

The second definitive question that should identify Christian counseling relates to the issue of a biblical world view: *Does the pastoral counselor take into account the reality of the spiritual world?* How does the fact that "Our struggle is not against flesh and blood, but against the rulers, against the authorities, against the powers of this dark world and against the spiritual forces of evil in the heavenly realms" (Ephesians 6:12, NIV) enter into our counseling procedure? How does a counselor lead a person from bondage to freedom? (This is the subject of my second book, *The Bondage Breaker.* These two books provide the theological basis for how the people, whose stories are told in this book, found their freedom in Christ.)

Demon Possession or Demonization?

Another issue concerns demon possession. Can a Christian be demon possessed? No question polarizes the Christian community more than this one, and the tragedy is that there is no absolutely biblical way to answer it. However, there are two things worthy of note: In the English translations, the term "demon possession" is derived from only one Greek word. Therefore, I prefer to use the word *demonized* instead. Also, the word translated as "demon possession" never occurs in Scripture after the cross, so we are left with no theological precision as to what demonization would constitute in the Church Age.

However, the fact that a Christian can be influenced to one degree or another by the "god of this world" is a New Testament given. If not, then why are we instructed to put on the armor of God and stand firm (Ephesians 6:10), to take every thought captive to the obedience of Christ (2 Corinthians 10:5), and to resist the devil (James 4:7)? And what if we don't put on the armor of God, stand firm, assume responsibility for what we think; and what if we fail to resist the devil? Then what? We are easy prey for the enemy of our souls.

So how can we tell if a problem is psychological or spiritual? I believe that question is basically false. Our problems are never not psychological. There is no time when previous experiences, personal relationships and our own mind, will and emotions are not contributing to our present problems or are the key to their resolution. But our problems are also never not spiritual. There is no time when God isn't here, nor is there a time when it is safe to take off the armor of God. The possibility of being tempted, accused and deceived by the evil one is a continuous reality. We must deal with the whole person, addressing both the spiritual and the psychological, or a counterfeit spirituality will take the place of true spirituality—such as the encroachment of New Age philosophy into twelve-step and other self-help recovery groups, secular psychology and education.

An Encounter of Truth or Power?

Next I'd like to talk about a procedural issue. I advocate what I call a "truth encounter" rather than a "power encounter." The classic model for deliverance is to summon the expert who will call up the demon, get its name and sometimes rank, and then cast it out. In a power encounter, the struggle is between an outside agent and the demonic stronghold. But it's not power that sets the captive free; it's truth (John 8:32). Living in defeat, believers often falsely conclude that they need power, so they look for some religious experience that promises them power. There isn't a verse in the Bible after Pentecost that encourages us to seek power, only the truth. That's because the power of the Christian lies in the truth; we already possess all the power we need because we are in Christ. The problem is that we don't see or believe it, and that is why the apostle Paul prays that we might come to this understanding (Ephesians 1:18,19). In contrast, the power of Satan is in the lie and once you expose the lie, you break his power.

In a truth encounter, I deal only with the person, and I do not bypass the person's mind. In that way people are free to make their own choices. There is never a loss of control as I facilitate the process of helping them assume their own responsibility before God. After all, it isn't what I say, do or believe that sets people free—it's what they renounce, confess, forsake, whom they forgive and the truth they affirm that sets them free. This "truth procedure" requires me to work with the whole person, dealing with body, soul and spirit.

Medicine and the Church

Treating the whole person includes the physical and interpersonal. Of course, there are glandular problems and chemical imbalances, and the church and the medical field should covet one another's contributions. The medical profession positions itself to heal the body, but only the church is in any position to resolve the spiritual conflicts. So let's not sit in judgment of the shortcomings of the secular world if we as the church are not assuming our responsibility for spiritual resolution.

In these last days we are going to see many spiritual counterfeits. In *Walking Through the Darkness*, I try to identify those counterfeits and establish parameters of divine guidance. We need that kind of spiritual discernment to stand against the New Age philosophies and false teachers who will rise among us (2 Peter 2:1f). The primary proponents of wholistic medicine are New Agers, and the majority of health food stores are staffed by them. There is nothing wrong with the pills on the shelves; just don't read the literature on the racks.

Satan's Greatest Access

Also, our problems never originate, nor are they resolved, in isolation from relationships. We absolutely need God, but we also desperately need each other. In my experience, unforgiveness of others affords the greatest access Satan has to the church. When people forgive from the heart, they take a giant step toward freedom. And once they are free, good relationships help nurture them toward growth. That's why, for example, resolving a child's spiritual problem only to send him back into a dysfunctional family is not an adequate solution. (Steve Russo and I have dealt with this at length in our book, *The Seduction of Our Children.*)

No Instant Maturity

The last issue is distinguishing between freedom and maturity. I don't believe in instant maturity. It takes time to renew our minds, develop character and learn to live responsible lives. But a captive first needs to be set free, and then he needs to learn how to enjoy that freedom, for it was for freedom that Christ set us free (Galatians 5:1). In my experience, bound people don't grow and seldom, if ever, do they experience emotional healing. A bound person needs to be released and a wounded person needs to be treated with compassion so they can be healed over time.

Now, let me introduce you to some choice followers of Christ. As they share their life stories, I will add some insights about the nature of their problems and their resolutions. You will learn at least as much from their experiences as you will from my comments. It's my prayer that their testimonies will be a tremendous encouragement, both to those who are longing to be free and to those who desire to help them.

1

Molly:
Freedom From the Cycle of Abuse

I like to start a conference by asking the people, "In the short time that I am here, if I really got to know you, would I like you? I mean, if I *really* got to know you?" I asked my seminary class that question and before I could go on, one of my students responded, "You'd feel sorry for me!" It was said in humor, but it captured the perspective of many who live a life of quiet desperation. Lost in their loneliness and self-pity, they cling to a thin thread of hope that somehow God will break through the fog of despair surrounding their life.

The system has not been kind to them. The parents who were to provide the nurturing love and acceptance they needed were instead the cause of their plight. The church they clung to for hope didn't seem to have the answers.

Such is the case of our first story. I had never met Molly before I received a rather lengthy letter sharing her new-found freedom in Christ. Then, months later on a conference tour, I had the privilege to meet her. I expected to see a broken-down, dumpy human being. But instead, the person who had lunch with my wife and me was a thoroughly professional, intelligent and attractive woman.

You will form your own mental picture as you meet her yourself. Her story is important because I didn't personally counsel her. She found her freedom by watching the videos of our conference on "Resolving Personal and Spiritual Conflicts" in Sunday school. Her story is representative of those who suffer because of a dysfunctional family and an inept church. I believe that many who are in spiritual bondage would step into freedom today if they knew who they are in Christ and what is the nature of the spiritual battle going on for their mind. Jesus Christ is the deliverer, and He has come to give abundant life.

*   *   *

Molly's Story

*I was born to the two meanest people
I have ever met.*

My whole life has changed since I became involved in the video series on "Resolving Personal and Spiritual Conflicts." The source of my lifelong bondages became clear to me for the first time. I am forty years old, and I feel that I have just now reached the "promised land."

I was born in a rural area, grass roots U.S.A., to the two meanest people I have ever met. My father was a farmer with very little education who married my mother very young. My father was one of fifteen children in a family plagued with mental illness. There is a lot of instability in my mother's family as well, but they simply deny there is a problem.

The bright spot among my relatives was my grandmother. I'm sure I would have gone over the edge long ago if it had not been for her. She was a saint and I knew she loved me.

I was the firstborn of my parents, but that was after they had been married for twelve years. My first memory of them together is that of my mom locking my dad outside at night. I can still see the fierce expression on his face as he looked at me through the door and yelled, "Molly! Open the door and let me in." My mom, who was standing directly behind me, screamed, "Don't you dare open that door."

> *I could see, at the end of the bed,*
> *that classic devil character.*

My mother and father divorced when I was four and my mother moved us out of the house. Sometime before the divorce, I remember one evening when my mother and father were planning to go out. My one-year-old sister and I were in their bed, probably waiting for a babysitter, when suddenly I saw an evil appearance that was *exactly* like the classic red devil, dancing at the end of the bed. I was petrified with fear and felt compelled not to tell anyone exactly what I was seeing.

I called for my mother, crying as I told her only that there was something in the room. She turned the light on and said, "There's nothing here; there's nothing here." I pulled up the covers so I couldn't see the end of the bed as she turned out the light and went out of the room. I stayed hidden under the bed covers for a long time, afraid to look out. When I did, the presence was still there, laughing.

> *Those words felt like a knife going*
> *through my heart.*

After my mother and father divorced, I remember the two of them meeting on the street, stopping to chat, and my daddy asking my mother if he could have my sister. Those words felt like a knife going through my heart because they meant that my father did not want me.

The voices probably started right then: "Your father doesn't even want you." And it was true. He told me all through my life that I was "just like my mother." I knew what that meant; I knew he hated her. She was a "rageaholic," and I was terrorized by her outbursts of anger.

One time when I was about six, I was at my dad's house and an aunt said to him, "Molly looks exactly like you." Instantly, his whole demeanor changed, and he stood up and screamed at her, "She looks exactly like her mother! I lived with that woman for sixteen years and she looks like her mother!" With that, he stomped out of the house, and I felt a sharp pain shoot through my chest.

I was so afraid she would poison us.

Members of our family thought my mother might harm us. One time when my mother was really bad, an aunt came to our home and stood outside one of our windows. She was watching over us because she worried about our safety. Mother cursed us a lot of the time and totally controlled our lives. She had no friends, no love or tenderness, and often said that her life would have been a lot better without me. I felt she resented us and we were a bother to her.

In the next couple of years, Mom became even more bitter and mean. For the remainder of my years with her, I feared for my life. Though I didn't know much about the spiritual world, I felt, even then, that Satan was involved in our home life.

Finally there came a time when I would not eat my food unless my mother ate hers first because I was so afraid she would poison us. I can't describe the terror of being a child and always living with a foreboding threat of danger. Though some of our relatives feared for us as well, they feared her more, so they never did anything about it.

Once when I was fourteen, my mother decided that I'd lost something and she refused to listen when I tried to tell her that I never had the thing. She beat and cursed me from six in the evening until one in the morning, making me go from room to room and even outside in the dark to go through the trash, searching over and over again for this item. I guess she finally got tired and went to bed. The thing I was looking for was the top to the toothpaste tube!

Right after that, my dad came for his monthly visit. He probably would have seen us more, but his wife ranted and raved the whole time they were with us, treating us much the same way our mother did. On the way home that day, my mind suddenly blanked out. I could not remember who I was or who all the people in the car were. A huge lump welled up in my throat, and I was so scared that I couldn't talk. Then just as suddenly, when Dad turned onto our street, my memory came flooding back. Oh, how I hated walking back into the "hell" of my home, but there was nowhere else to go.

Through all of this, I desperately wanted the love of my father and mother. All the way into my thirties, I called my mom every day even though she would often slam the phone in my ear. I was still trying to get her to love me.

He always threatened to tell my mother that I was smoking cigarettes if I told her what he did.

When I was quite young, one of my uncles, who had a number of children of his own, would come over to our house and take me out. Apparently, it never occurred to my mother to be cautious and question why he would do that. From the time I was four until I was seven, I remember him fondling me and threatening to tell my mother that I was smoking cigarettes if I told her what he did. I remember feeling tremendous guilt, thinking that I should have said "no," but was afraid to do it.

After that I became addicted to masturbation, a problem that I never could control until I found my freedom in Christ. That sexual desire has tried to come back, but now I know what to do about it. I just proclaim aloud that I am a child of God and tell Satan and his evil emissaries to leave me. The compulsion is gone, instantly.

Recently I wanted to tell someone about that sexual addiction so that I would be accountable. When I did tell one of my friends who went to the Bible study I was attending, she said, "I've always had that problem, too." We cried together and I told her of my victory over that demonic influence and all of the violent sexual thoughts that went along with it. I rejoice now that I no longer have to be subject to the evil presence associated with that act and its overwhelming power. In Christ, I am free to choose not to sin in that way.

I was molested again at age nine by a business acquaintance of my mother. She let him take my sister and me for drives in his car and he would kiss me and put his tongue in my mouth. One time, I was so scared of what he might do that I crawled up in the back window of his car and begged him to take us home. After that, he stopped taking us out.

I had seen movies where people lost touch with reality.

Things became worse as I grew older. I don't remember when, but I started to pray that God would not let me lose my mind and end up in an institution. I knew that I could very easily because I had been hearing voices as long as I can remember. I had seen movies like *The Three Faces of Eve* where people lost touch with reality, and I could see how that could happen to me.

We had no spiritual life. My mother totally rejected Christianity and wouldn't let me talk about it with her. My dad went to church every Sunday, but was extremely legalistic—a trap I later fell into.

I began to attend a neighborhood church as a teenager and became very legalistic, doing everything they told me to do . . . everything . . . to make sure that I would be happy when I was older.

At the age of fourteen, I asked Jesus Christ to be my Savior, and I was so thrilled I couldn't wait to learn all that I could about Him. The first time I went to a youth group, they distributed some books and gave us an assignment to do. By the next week, I had answered all of the questions and purchased a notebook. Someone saw that I had completed the work and yelled out, "Look, everybody, she even answered the questions." The whole group laughed and I never did an assignment again.

Sunday school was worse. There were a lot of girls in our church who were wealthy, and everyone in our Sunday school class was in a sorority except me and one other girl. We would call each other every Sunday morning to be sure we would both be there because the others didn't talk to us, and neither of us wanted to be there alone.

All during this time the voices were saying, "You're

ugly. You're disgusting. You're unworthy. God couldn't possibly love you." My life seemed to have a way of making me believe that about myself.

When I got married, God would let me find happiness.

The oppression, depression and condemning voices continued, but no one knew. There was no one I could talk to. I thought I deserved it. When I tried to tell people what my mother was like, they either didn't understand or responded inappropriately. Once I confided in a Sunday school teacher and she said, "Let's go talk to your mother." That struck icy fear in my heart because I knew what I would get from my mother after the teacher left, so I wouldn't do it. I was too terrified.

I lived by a code of self-effort, trying to please my mother to keep her from becoming angry. I believed that God put me where I was, and if I could stand the suffering, be obedient, live a good life and not sin, then when I got married He would let me find happiness. My goal was to have a Christian home and a Christian husband so I could find happiness and a secure place where no one would abuse me.

Marriage was a big shock.

The summer after my graduation I ran into a man I had met at high school graduation, and it was love at first sight. He was the man I would marry for happiness ten months later, when I was nineteen. We were in church every Sunday and every Wednesday night, and we went to everything else there was to attend. But we had no friends and were never invited to anyone's home.

They didn't offer pre-marital counseling at our church and marriage was a big shock. I had saved myself for marriage, but I hated sex. Within a week, my husband began staying away, sometimes for a weekend. We moved into an apartment, and with the boxes still unpacked he simply left to play golf and be with his friends.

That was the final straw after a lifetime of never having felt loved by anyone. My self-esteem was so low that when I realized my husband didn't care anymore, I just went to bed and sank into a deep depression. Three weeks later, I felt convicted and got up. I thought, *How could he love me? He couldn't respect someone who clung to him and tried to hold on for dear life to his every move.* So I tried to change and make our marriage work. Somehow, we managed to stay together for fifteen years . . . fifteen years of conflict, rejection and pain . . . vacillating between living a legalistic pretence of Christianity and completely turning our backs on God.

I wasn't the kind of woman who was flirty.

I hoped that having a child would bring happiness, and when I couldn't get pregnant I started seeing doctors. When my fifty-year-old doctor was kind and held my hand, I felt he was just being fatherly. But then he fondled me while I was on the examination table. Later, when I developed a lump in my breast, I went to another doctor, and he did something similar.

I wasn't the kind of woman who is flirty; I could hardly look another person in the eye. I believe that is just the way Satan works, using others to bring his evil into our lives when we are vulnerable. I felt so very uncomfortable while these things were happening, but then I was used to being uncomfortable.

Later, one of my friends who worked in a law firm called and told me that one of those doctors had done the same thing to someone else and was being sued. That's when I finally knew that it wasn't me and I was relieved of some of my many doubts about myself. Right was wrong and wrong was right. My thought processes were so wrong that I just didn't know what was right.

I finally got pregnant and was catapulted into motherhood. Not very long after that, my husband came home one night and said, "All the guys at work talk about are girls and sex, so I spend most of my time with Linda. She goes to our church and she's a Christian and I go on breaks with her." He asked if I minded, and I said, "No, I don't mind." Eventually he left me for Linda.

My friends had warned me that he was seeing other women, but I wouldn't believe it. I just said, "He wouldn't do that." That was my way of dealing with it, because I wanted to avoid the pain of knowing or finding out that he was unfaithful.

I gave up on God.

When my husband finally walked out and left me with two babies, I gave up on God, blaming Him for all the pain. I learned in church that the way to happiness for a single girl is to marry a Christian, and I had done that. Now I was angry at God, and for six years I lived ignoring Him.

My mother urged me to "Do something. Don't just sit there with your life. Do something, even if it's wrong."

The people from work wanted me to go to the bar with them, and though I had never been to a bar, I went and soon got into that lifestyle. I never intended to date seamy people, but the lowest class of people would make me feel better. I even went to bars where some of the people had no teeth! I guess that was the only place I felt okay about myself because they were worse off than I was.

I was still bound by legalism and sometimes would try to go to church, but it took a Herculean effort. On Friday evenings I would go to the bar, and when my kids came home from visiting their father on Saturday, I would go back to being a good little mother. On Sunday I would try to take them to church, but when I did I felt like a nail was being driven into my temple. I had always had a lot of headaches, but this pain was excruciating. Sometimes I would get sick and have to leave, and once I threw up in the car, so I finally quit going to church.

I would go to the bar and someone would say something nice to me.

I remember one of the last sermons I heard. The preacher said, "There is a downward spiral. When it starts, the circle is really big and things are moving slow at the top. As it goes down, things are closer and closer together and go faster and faster until they are out of control. But you can stop the downward spiral by not taking that first step."

I took that first step. Things did get out of control and I couldn't stop. When I got depressed, I would go to the bar and someone would say something nice to me. I would have a drink and, temporarily, I didn't feel so bad. There was acceptance at the bar when there was very little of it in the church. I was in church regularly since I was fourteen, but never had a close friend. I was so withdrawn and it seemed like people didn't reach out, so I just sat there miserable and alone.

I was in such a bad place in my life. In those bars, people would get into knife fights and sometimes somebody would pull a gun. But as time passed I got to the place where I would even go in to drink by myself and ignore the danger. I really didn't care anymore what happened to me.

I remember saying, "I don't feel bad about this."

I had a brush with cancer which frightened me, and I thought maybe God was stomping on me. So I quit the bars and went back to church. But after a year I forgot my cancer scare and slipped into the old lifestyle. I was living such a lie that it was inevitable. I had always had a strong conscience before, but at that time I remember thinking, *I don't even feel bad about this.*

I was unhappy and miserable and thought of suicide, but I was such a chicken I couldn't do it. My life was so out of control that when I met a man at a bar who wanted to marry me, I rushed headlong into it. I didn't ask God what He thought about it, because I knew what His answer would be and I didn't care. The guy was still married when I met him and was a client where I worked. I was so afraid he would mention that he knew me from the bar—I wanted to keep that part of my life secret. I married him out of desperation to find happiness, but we were only together for two years.

Even before that marriage, I had slipped back into a legalistic cycle where I tried to control everything. We went to church, and I made sure my husband read everything I wanted him to read. But he was more sick than I was and very weak, with no sense of his own identity. In the beginning, I could control everything. But when his two daughters came to live with us, "all hell broke loose." Their mother had been in a mental hospital and was now living in a lesbian relationship. The girls were totally without discipline and I decided I was going to "save" them, but my efforts blew up in my face.

I asked my husband to leave because I knew he was planning to leave me anyway, and I wanted to get the jump on him. I filed for divorce, but then I couldn't sleep nights and I stopped the proceedings. I knew it was wrong. I told him that he could get the divorce if he wanted to, but I never heard from him again.

---

*We had gone to counselors,
but nobody helped us.*

My second husband and I did go to counseling, but no one was able to help us. They didn't deal with the reality of spiritual conflict, so how could they help us? They just patted us on the hand and said everything would be all right.

Finally my last counselor did acknowledge that I was having a spiritual problem. I told him repeatedly about the fear of dying . . . about the suicide thoughts . . . about never being able to feel loved by God . . . about the cloud that overwhelmed me when I came home . . . but he didn't seem to know how to help me.

He asked me if I loved God, and I said, "I don't know."

He responded, "Well, I know you do." I told him that the only God I knew was up in the heavens with a hammer waiting to beat me. He argued with me that God was not like that, but it didn't help.

I didn't tell him about the big black spider I saw as I woke up in the mornings, because after I started the day I forgot about it. It's incredible that this went on about ten years and I never thought about it except while it was happening. Then I convinced myself I was having a nightmare with my eyes open.

Finally I couldn't stand pretending anymore. I would cry all weekend and pray, "God, I can't pretend anymore that I'm okay." I would get up when the kids came home from their weekend and put on my good-mother face. The truth was that all weekend I had laid on the couch in utter blackness. I didn't open the windows and I never went out. And I never talked to anybody because there were always the voices: "They don't want to talk with you. They don't like you." I never realized the negative things I heard in my head were put there by Satan.

---

*It was like a cloud was waiting there
to engulf me.*

I would do okay at work, but the second I walked in the door at night a cloud was waiting there to engulf me. I would usually just lay on the couch again, feeling miserable. Menial things like going to the grocery were really difficult because people were out there, and I felt they all hated me.

I kept going to the last counselor because I was desperate and couldn't keep up the pretence any longer. I was even crying at work. I told the counselor, "I'm losing my mind. I'm miserable. I can't go on."

He gave me a book to read, but it never got to the core of the problem. Although it spoke of Christ, there was no resolution; there was only hope if you could go to one of the clinics it described. However, the book did refer to malignant co-dependency and I knew that was me: no friends, totally isolated, living a lie, not knowing who I was. That petrified me.

After I read the book, I went to my counselor and said, "This is me . . . " I was on the verge of suicide, but he simply told me to come back in two weeks. I tried to get into the clinic but couldn't because I didn't have the money they required.

My sister was also going through serious problems at the time, but she couldn't go to the counselor at our church because she wasn't a member. They were so overloaded they couldn't take non-members. My counselor recommended a class for children of dysfunctional families at another church. I wanted to go too, but it was hard to start over with a new group of people.

When the weekend came, my children went away and I laid on the couch all Friday night and all day Saturday, totally depressed and eating nothing but popcorn. By Sunday the thought came that I should attend the class. Nothing in the world could have been harder to do, but somehow I gathered the courage to go. When I walked into that class, I felt totally at home. I attended regularly and it helped a lot. It was so good to have friends even though they were sick themselves.

As I viewed the video, my mouth fell open.

One of my new friends invited me to a different class where they were showing the video series by Neil Anderson. As I viewed the video, my mouth fell open and I found myself saying repeatedly, "This is the truth." After that, I wouldn't have missed that class for anything. Once I went sick because nothing in my life had given me such hope.

When I heard Neil talk about people hearing voices, I was so excited because I'd finally found someone who knew what I was experiencing. Then he talked about Zechariah 3, where Satan is accusing the high priest and the Lord says, "I rebuke you Satan." And that truth set me free. I thought, *I can do that.*

I realized then that I had been deceived by the father

of lies, Satan. He has been accusing me all my life and I did not stand against him. I learned that because I am in the Lord Jesus Christ, I have authority to rebuke deceiving spirits and reject Satan's lies. I left that evening floating on air.

The depression is gone . . . the voices are gone . . . that huge spider-like object that I have been seeing in my room for the past ten years when I first wake up is gone!

I love the light now.

My employer gave me the "Resolving Personal and Spiritual Conflicts" tape series for Christmas, and I have been listening to them over and over again. There's light in my mind where there was darkness before. I love the light now and open the curtains and windows to let it shine in. I really am a new person! I have people into my home for a Bible study with the tapes, something I couldn't have done before.

As I look back over my life, I see that the messages I got from my family were negative. I can't remember really feeling love in my life until I heard the video tapes and realized God loves me just as I am.

Before I found my freedom in Christ, I was behaving just as my mother before me, going into rages with my kids and then hating myself afterwards. That is so rare now, and my children feel comfortable with me.

I'm not like I was; I'm being healed. When I see myself falling back into old habit or thought patterns, I know what to do. I don't have to grovel in self-pity. At each point of conflict I can look for the particular lie Satan wants me to believe and then stand against it by deliberately choosing what I now know to be true.

My great goal now is to be the kind of parent God wants me to be, and I believe He will make up for all of the years the locusts have eaten (Joel 2:24,25).

*   *   *

How People Live

Nobody can consistently behave in a way that is inconsistent with how they perceive themselves. Molly believed she wasn't any good, that nobody wanted her, that she wasn't worthy of love. She was living a distorted life, foisted on her by abused and abusive parents. The cycle of abuse would have continued except for the grace of God.

When I hear a story like this, and I hear a lot of them, I just wish people like Molly could be hugged by someone in a healthy way for every time they have been touched wrongly. I want to apologize to her for her parents. I want to see people have a chance. They are sitting in bars near your church. Some sneak in the back door of the sanctuary and sit in the last row. Others become clinging pests whom we seek to avoid. They are children of God, but they don't know it and most have never been treated as such.

Stopping the Abuse Cycle

We Christians have all the power we need to live productive lives and the authority to resist the devil. People like Molly are not the problem; they are the victims—victimized by the god of this world, abusive parents, a cruel society and legalistic or liberal churches.

How do we stop this cycle of abuse? We lead them to Christ and help them establish their identity as children of God. We teach them the reality of the spiritual world, and encourage them to walk by faith in the power of the Holy Spirit. We care enough to confront them in love and stand by them when they fall. We do it by becoming the pastors, parents and friends that God wants us to be. We pay attention to the words of Christ in Matthew 9:12,13:

> It is not those who are healthy who need a physician, but those who are sick. But go and learn what this means, "I desire compassion, and not sacrifice," for I did not come to call the righteous, but sinners.

The "Steps to Freedom in Christ" that helped Molly as

she viewed the video tapes are given in the appendix. They can also be found in *The Bondage Breaker.*

The Path to God

In no way am I advocating a quick fix for difficult problems. Just going through seven simple steps or prayers may seem simplistic or easy, but I would beg to differ. There are a million ways to go wrong. The road to destruction is broad, the paths numerous and their explanation complex. But the path back to God is not so broad. Jesus is the way which is narrow, the truth which is simple, and the life which is transforming. No wonder Paul said, "I am afraid, lest as the serpent deceived Eve by his craftiness, your minds should be led astray from the simplicity and purity of devotion to Christ" (2 Corinthians 11:3).

However, helping a person to recognize deception and counterfeit guidance and to choose the truth isn't simple. Knowing how to get a person in touch with the emotional pain of the past and work through forgiveness isn't easy. Confronting a person about pride, rebellion and sinful behavior requires a lot of unconditional love and acceptance.

Some are able to process these steps on their own as Molly did. My son asked me once if people could effect their own freedom in Christ. Yes they can, because truth is what sets us free and Jesus is the deliverer. However, many are going to need the assistance of a godly person. Prerequisites for the pastor/counselor are the character of Christ and the knowledge of His ways. This type of counseling requires the presence and leading of the Holy Spirit who is the "Wonderful Counselor."

It seems as though the majority of the helping professions focus on the problem. We are suffering from a paralysis of analysis. If I were lost in a maze, I wouldn't want someone to explain to me all the intricacies of mazes and why people stumble into them. I certainly wouldn't need someone to tell me what a jerk I was for getting in there in the first place. I would need and want someone to give me a road map out of there. God sent His Son as our Savior, provided the

Scriptures as a road map and sent the Holy Spirit to guide us. People all around us are dying in the maze of life, for want of someone to gently show them the way.

2

Anne:
Freedom Through Stages of Growth

Molly has shared her life, and I hope it has impacted yours. In the following chapters we will benefit from the stories of other courageous people who have allowed their stories to be told.

However, this chapter will be a little different. Before we go on, I believe it is important to see God's growth and sanctification process, both explained from the Scriptures and illustrated in the life of another restored person, Anne. This will help you to better understand the spiritual journeys of the people you will be meeting here and how you can help heal the hurting lives of those who cross your path.

Born Dead

Paul writes, "As for you, you were dead in your transgressions and sins, in which you used to live when you followed the ways of this world and of the ruler of the kingdom of the air, the spirit who is now at work in those who are disobedient" (Ephesians 2:1,2, NIV). Since Adam, we are all born physically alive but spiritually dead (i.e., separated from God). During our formative years, we learned how to live our lives independent of God. We had neither the presence of God in our lives nor the knowledge of God's ways.

This learned independence from God is characteristic of

the flesh or old nature. And one of the ways the flesh functions is to develop defense mechanisms whereby we learn how to cope, succeed, survive or win without God.

Eternally Alive

When we come to Christ, we become spiritually alive, which means that we are now in union with God. Eternal life is not something we receive when we die; we possess eternal life right now because we are *in* Christ: "The witness is this, that God has given us eternal life, and this life is in His Son. He who has the Son has the life; he who does not have the Son of God does not have the life" (1 John 5:11,12).

Reprogrammed

At the moment of conversion, all of God's resources are available to us. Unfortunately, nobody pushes the "clear" button in our previously programmed minds. Until God's transformation process begins in our lives, we live in a state of being conformed to this world and regimented by it. That's why Paul writes, "Do not conform any longer to the pattern of this world, but be transformed by the renewing of your mind. Then you will be able to test and approve what God's will is—His good, pleasing and perfect will" (Romans 12:2, NIV). Therefore—

- the major task of Christian education is to disciple previously programmed people, living independent of God, into a dependant relationship with Him.
- the major task of discipleship/counseling is to free people from their past and eradicate old defense mechanisms by substituting Christ as their only defense.

Becoming Transformed

Truth and obedience are key issues in living a Christ-dependent lifestyle. But truth can only be believed if it is understood, and commandments can only be obeyed if they are known. As the Holy Spirit leads us into all truth, we must respond by trusting and obeying: "The one who says, 'I have come to know Him,' and does not keep His commandments, is a liar, and the truth is not in him" (1 John 2:4). Disobedience allows Satan to work in us. According to Ephesians 2:2, that spirit "is now at work in those who are disobedient" (NIV).

"Sanctification" is the name applied to the process of our becoming conformed into the image and character of Christ. God is at work in this process, patiently and gently moving us along, because it takes time to renew our minds and develop character. But another god is also active—to see this process as taking place independent of the "the ruler of the kingdom of the air" (the god of this world, Satan) would be a disastrous oversight.

Diffusing the Past

In many cases, traumatic childhood experiences continue to have a debilitating effect upon present living. It is very common to have many of these experiences blocked from memory. Secular psychologists are aware of this and attempt to get at hidden memories through hypnosis. Some try a hospitalization program using drugs to induce memories. While their sincerity is commendable, I am unequivocally opposed to both procedures for two reasons: One, I don't want to do anything to bypass the mind of a person; and two, I don't want to get ahead of God's timing.

You will find no instruction in Scripture to dwell on yourself or direct your thoughts inward. Scripture always argues for the active use of our minds and for our thoughts to be directed outward. We invite God to search our hearts (Psalms 139:23,24). All occultic practices will try to induce a passive state of the mind, and Eastern religions will admonish us to bypass it. Scripture requires us to think and assume responsibility for taking every thought captive to the obedience of Christ (2 Corinthians 10:5).

If there are hurtful ways within us, and hidden memories of our past, God will wait until we reach enough maturity before He reveals them. Paul says:

I care very little if I am judged by you or by any human court; indeed, I do not even judge myself. My conscience is clear, but that does not make me innocent. It is the Lord who judges me. Therefore judge nothing before the appointed time; wait till the Lord comes. He will bring to light what is hidden in darkness and will expose the motives of men's hearts. At that time each will receive his praise from God (1 Corinthians 4:3-5, NIV).

Pursuing God

What should we do if we know something in our past is still affecting us? I believe we should continue the pursuit of knowing God, learn to believe and obey that which is true, and commit ourselves to the sanctifying process of developing character. When we have reached enough security and maturity in Christ, He reveals a little more about who we really are. As Christ becomes the only defense we need, He weans us of our old means of defending ourselves.

Stripping off old defense mechanisms and revealing character deficiencies is like taking off layers of an onion. When one layer is off, we feel great. We have nothing against ourselves, and we are free from what others think about us, but we have not yet fully arrived. At the right time, He reveals more in order that we may share in His holiness.

Our next story is about this progressive process of sanctification. Anne wrote me the following letter and handed it to me halfway through a conference. She heard who she was as a child of God, learned how to walk by faith and saw the nature of the battle for her mind. She was so excited that she jumped ahead and processed the Steps to Freedom on her own.

*   *   *

Dear Neil:

Praise God, I think this is the answer I've been searching for. I'm not crazy! I don't have an overactive imagination as I have been told and believed for years. I'm just normal like everybody else.

How could I admit to someone in the church what had crossed my mind?

I have struggled for my whole Christian experience with bizarre thoughts that were so embarrassing I usually never told anyone else. How could I admit to someone in the church what had crossed my mind? I tried once to honestly share part of what I was struggling with in a Christian group. People sucked in their breath, there was a stiff silence, then someone changed the subject. I could have died. I learned quickly that these things are not acceptable in the church, or at least they weren't at that time.

I didn't know what it meant to take every thought captive.[1] I tried to do this once, but I was unsuccessful because I blamed myself for all this stuff. I thought all those thoughts were mine and that I was the one who was doing it. There has always been a terrible cloud hanging over my head because of these issues. I never could accept the fact that I was really righteous because I didn't feel like it.

Praise God it was only Satan—not me. I have worth!! The problem is so easy to deal with when you know what it is.

I was abused as a child. My mother lied to me a lot and Satan used the things she said, like, "You're lazy. You'll never amount to anything." Over and over he has been feeding me so much junk—preying on my worst fears. At night I would have nightmares that the lies were true and in the morning I would be so depressed. I have had a difficult time shaking this stuff.

Being abused, I was taught not to think for myself. I did what I was told and never questioned anything for fear of being beaten. This set me up for Satan's mind games. I was conditioned to have someone lie to me about myself, primarily my mother. I feared taking control of my mind because I didn't know what would happen. I believed I

---

1. Anne gives a good description of what it means to "take every thought captive," when, later in her letter, she says, "I just need to examine the thought according to the Word of God and then choose the truth."

would lose my identity because I wouldn't have anyone to tell me what to do.

Now I'm finally me, a child of God!

In actuality, I have gained my identity for the first time. I am not a product of my mother's lies; I am not a product of the garbage Satan feeds me. Now I'm finally me, a child of God! Through all his junk, Satan has terrorized me. I have been living in fear of myself, but praise God I think it's over. I used to worry whether a thought came from Satan or myself. Now I realize that's not the issue. I just need to examine the thought according to the Word of God and then choose the truth.

I feel a little unsure writing this so soon. Maybe I should take a "wait and see" attitude, but I am sensing such joy and peace that I feel in my gut it must be real. Praise God for the truth and answered prayer! I am free!

With a heart full of thanks,

Anne

*   *   *

One layer of the onion was exposed. The critical first part of the Epistles, which speaks of our identity in Christ, was made known to Anne. She is no longer just a product of her past; she is a new creation in Christ. With that foundation laid, she was able to face and repudiate the lies she had believed for so many years. When she had tried to share some of her struggles in the past, she had felt rejected, probably because others in the group were struggling in a similar fashion but were unable to reciprocate.

Oh, how I long for the day when our churches will help people firmly establish their identity in Christ and provide an atmosphere where people like Anne could share the real nature of their struggle. Satan does everything in the dark. When issues like this arise, let's not suck in our breath and change the subject. We buy Satan's devious strategy by keeping everything hidden. Let's walk in the light, and have fellowship with one another in order that the blood of Jesus will cleanse us from all sin (1 John 1:7). God is light and in Him there is no darkness at all (1 John 1:5). Let's lay aside falsehood and speak the truth in love, for we are members of one another (Ephesians 4:15,25).

Now Anne knows who she is and understands the nature of the battle going on for her mind. She must be totally free, right? Wrong! She was free of what she processed, but God wasn't through with her yet. One layer doesn't constitute the whole onion. Two weeks after the conference she wrote a second letter.

*   *   *

Dear Neil:

Good night! Where do I start? Let me just say that I came to your conference for academic reasons. I could not have fathomed in advance what the Lord had in store for me. In fact, I probably wouldn't have believed it anyway. I guess I should start where I left off with you a few days ago.

I wrote you a letter explaining that I had been freed from obsessive thoughts. A few months ago, I had specifically asked the Lord to help me understand this problem. When I heard the information in the conference at the beginning of the week, I was thrilled. It was exactly what I had asked the Lord for. At home, I prayed through all of the prayers in the Steps to Freedom. It was a struggle, but the voices stopped. I felt free; thus, I thought I was done. Little did I know!

> ### As a result of that phony effort, I became very bitter and sarcastic.

You talked to me one evening after a session and told me that I probably needed to forgive my mother. I didn't buy it very well because I had tried it once before and it didn't work. I now realize that I was pushed into it by some well-meaning Christians who said that my feelings didn't matter. In fact, they said I shouldn't even have any angry feelings. To them, the kind of rage I was feeling was very sinful. So I grudgingly went through the motions of saying that I forgave the people who had hurt me. As a result of that phony effort, I became very bitter and sarcastic. I tried not to be, but the truth is that I was. God showed me later that my bitterness resulted from denying that I was angry while going through the motions of forgiving.

A year ago, I attended a support group for abuse victims. The leader of the group told me that I was bitter because I had tried to forgive before I was ready. She said that I needed to work through all of my feelings I had about each incident. After that, I would be able to forgive.

When you talked to me that evening, I thought you were coercing me into another ritual prayer of forgiveness that would mean nothing. All I knew was that I couldn't return to the bitterness trail. I decided to just take the information that I received at the beginning of the conference as what God wanted me to receive and put the rest of the information on the academic shelf.

The forgiveness issue hit me again.

Thursday evening, when you spoke on forgiveness, I was miserable. I had a horrible time sitting through the meeting, feeling bored and angry. I felt very misunderstood and thought I was wasting my time. I knew I couldn't leave or everybody would think I was possessed or something, so I struggled with staying awake and couldn't wait to get out of there.

That night, I started working on an assignment for a class I was taking. I couldn't process anything because the forgiveness issue hit me square in the face again. I felt angry, but something in my gut told me that there had to be something more to what you were saying. I decided that I should be open and willing to try anything. I figured it couldn't hurt, although I really doubted that it would help since I had been trying to forgive my parents for years.

So I made a list of people and offenses and worked

through them as you had suggested that night. During that time, God showed me that I had been hanging onto their offenses in anger because it was my way of protecting myself against further abuse. I didn't know how to scripturally set boundaries around myself to protect myself from them. I had been taught by the church that I must keep turning the other cheek and keep letting them slap it. When you spoke of what it really meant to honor your parents, I knew that was my ticket to freedom.

God showed me that it was okay to stick up for myself and that I didn't need an unforgiving attitude to protect myself. He showed me that the abuse support group was right in telling me to focus on my emotions; however, there was never any real closure because they never taught us to come to a decision about forgiveness. That was always down the road when you felt better. I see now that both Christian groups were emphasizing one aspect about forgiveness, but not both.

After forgiving, I felt exhausted. Interestingly, though, I immediately had a real love-jump in my heart for you, Neil. It hadn't been there before. I went to sleep feeling pretty good.

An hour later, I woke up with cold sweats and my heart racing. I had just had another one of my awful nightmares. I hadn't had one in several months, so I was kind of surprised. For the first time in my life, it occurred to me that maybe this wasn't all a result of my abuse as I had been taught in the past. I prayed that the Lord would help me figure it out and went back to sleep. At 2:30 A.M., my roommate woke me up with her screaming. I jumped out of bed and woke her up. We compared notes and realized we both had had similar dreams. After praying together and renouncing Satan,[2] we went back to bed and both slept fine the rest of the night.

In those early morning hours as I was drifting back to sleep, God showed me that I had been having similar dreams since third grade—dreams that I had met the devil and he had put a curse on me. I can't believe I forgot all that. I asked the Lord what happened in the third grade

---

2. Renouncing Satan is verbally standing against him as we are taught in James 4:7: "Resist the devil, and he will flee from you" (NIV).

and remembered that I had started watching *Bewitched* at that time. It was my favorite TV show and I watched it religiously.

Because of that show, I became very interested in spiritual powers. Along with many of my school friends, I read books on ghosts, E.S.P., palm reading, and even a book on spells and curses. It also was an "in" thing to play with magic eight balls, Ouija boards and magic sets. Another TV favorite was *Gilligan's Island,* where I got the idea to use my dolls as voodoo dolls to get back at my mother. I considered putting a curse on her. By the time I was in sixth grade, I was so depressed. I started reading Edgar Allan Poe and it became the only thing I craved. I can't believe I had forgotten all this.

In high school the dreams came back and I became suicidal. By the grace of God, I invited Jesus Christ into my life soon after that. The biggest thing God showed me was that I knew when I was very young that there was evil power out there, and I had desired to have it.

When Saturday came, you can bet I was all ears. This wasn't hocus-pocus to me anymore. So as you led us through the Steps to Freedom, I prayed all the prayers again and renounced all of the lies that have been going on in my family for years. I acknowledged my own sin and lack of forgiveness.

The best way I can describe what happened to me this week is this: You know how it is when somebody has been in a cult for a long time, and they get taken in for deprogramming? That's the way it was for me. It was like God locked me in a room and said, "Give me your brain. We're not leaving here until you do." It's taken an intensive week to get me to see the lies I have been living in. I had no idea.

---

*I could feel the oppression lifting
off my heart.*

Since I have returned home, the lying thoughts— "You're no good. You're stupid. No one likes you."—have been coming out in great numbers. I told my husband everything, so every time I have a lying thought I tell him and we both laugh about it and talk about what's really true. Praise God! I was too embarrassed to tell him before.

Last night one of my nightmares started up again. I felt the oppression coming on as I was drifting off to sleep. I said "Jesus" right away. Neil, I could feel the oppression lifting off my heart, quickly, almost like it had been torn away. Praise God!

Because of counseling through the years, I have quite a few notebooks filled with accounts of the pain from my past. This pain pile has been sitting in my drawer and has been an eyesore every time I have looked at it. I now know that my identity isn't in the past anymore; it's in Christ. I burned all the notebooks.

Thank you for telling me the truth even if I didn't understand it at first. The joy I feel is the same joy I felt when I first received Christ! Finally I understand what it means to be a child of God.

Joyfully,

Anne

*   *   *

Three layers of the onion peeled off in a week is rather remarkable. Anne saw her identity in Christ, was able to forgive from her heart and learned to stand against Satan. She may have more going for her than most, having a Christian education and a loving, understanding and supportive husband to go home to. That is not to say that others can't resolve the same issues, but for some it may take longer.

Forgiveness Brings Freedom

Several issues need to be brought out. Every person in this book has had to face the need to forgive. It drives legitimate counselors up a wall when well-meaning Christians suggest that somebody who expresses feelings like anger and bitterness shouldn't "feel that way." Bypassing feelings will never bring resolution to problems. If you want healing, you will have to get in touch with your emotional core. God will surface the emotional pain in order that it may be dealt with. Those who don't want to face reality will try to shove it down, but that will only result in increased bitterness.

Forgiveness is what sets us free from our past. We don't do it for the other person's sake; we do it for our sake. We are to forgive as Christ has forgiven us. There is no freedom without forgiveness. "But you don't know how bad they hurt me," says the victim. The point is, they're still hurting you, so how do you stop the pain? You need to forgive from the heart—acknowledge the hurt and the hate and then let it go. To not forgive from the heart is to give Satan an opportunity (Matthew 18:34,35; 2 Corinthians 2:10,11).

Another error is to see forgiveness as a long-term process. Many counselors say, "You will have to feel all the emotion, then you will be able to forgive." Going over the past and reliving all the pain without forgiveness only reinforces it. The more you talk about it, the stronger the hold it has upon you. The assumption seems to be that you have to heal first, then you will be able to forgive. Not true! You forgive first, then the healing process can begin.

There is no way that you can read Scripture and come to the conclusion that forgiveness is a long-term process. The painful feelings may take time to heal, but forgiveness is a choice. It is a crisis of the will and the reward is freedom.

Stand Against Sin

Many, like Anne, see their anger as a means of protecting themselves from further abuse. Secular counselors see Christian forgiveness as co-dependency and argue, "Don't let that person shove you around anymore. Get mad!" I say, "Don't let that person shove you around anymore. Forgive!"

Then take a stand against sin. Forgiveness is not tolerating ways in which others may be sinning against you. God forgives, but He doesn't tolerate sin. It grieves me that some pastors will hear of abuse and tell the child or wife to just go home and submit, saying, "Trust God to protect you." I want to say to that pastor, "You go home in the place of that person and get knocked around." But doesn't the Bible say that wives and children are to be submissive? True, but it also says that God has established government to protect abused children and battered wives. Read Romans 13:1-7, and turn abusers in as the law even requires you to do in many states.

If a man in your church abused another woman in your church, would you tolerate it? If a man or woman in your church abused another person's child, would you tolerate that? Why, then, would you allow in your own home what is so clearly an intolerable sin in others, just because you are the wife or child?

Parents are charged by God to love, protect and provide for their household. Never are they given a license to abuse, nor should it ever be tolerated. Turn them in, for everyone's sake. It isn't helping the abuser to let him or her continue in sin.

One mother of three shared with me in tears one evening that she knew exactly who it was that she needed to forgive. It was her mother. But if she forgave her that evening, what was she to do that Sunday when she had to go over to her house? "She will just bad-mouth me all over again." I said, "Put a stop to it. Maybe you should say something like, 'Listen Mom, you have been bad-mouthing me all my life. It isn't doing you any good and it certainly isn't doing me any good. I really can't be a part of that anymore. If you have to treat me that way then I'm going to leave.'"

Her response was typical: "Doesn't the Bible say that I am suppose to honor my mother?" I explained that letting her mother systematically destroy her and her present family would certainly not honor her mother. Eventually it would dishonor her.

"Honor your mother and father" is better understood as taking financial care of them in their old age. The need to obey one's parents no longer applies to this woman since she had left her mother and father and was now under the authority of her husband.

Living With Consequences

The major decision you are making in forgiveness is to

bear the penalty of the other person's sin. All forgiveness is efficacious. If we are to forgive as Christ forgave us, how then did He forgive? He took the sins of the world on Himself; He suffered the consequences of our sin. When we forgive the sin of another, we are agreeing to live with the consequences of his or her sin. You say, "That's not fair!" Well, the fact is that you will have to anyway, whether you forgive or not. Everybody is living with the consequences of somebody else's sin. We are all living with the consequences of Adam's sin. The only real choice is whether we will do it in the freedom of forgiveness or the bondage of bitterness.

You might ask, "Why should I let them off my hook?" The point is that when you have them on your hook, you are also hooked to them through your unforgiveness. One man exclaimed, "That's why moving away didn't resolve it." When you let them off your hook, are they off God's? Never! God says, "Vengeance is mine. I will repay" (Hebrews 10:30). God will deal justly with everyone in the final judgment.

Get God Into the Process

We need to get God into the process. Step Three in the Steps to Freedom addresses Bitterness versus Forgiveness, and begins with a prayer asking God to reveal "to my mind those people I have not forgiven in order that I may do so." I have had many look at me in all sincerity and say they don't think there is anyone they need to forgive. But I ask them to share with me names that are coming to their mind anyway. Within minutes, I often have a full page of names because the Lord is faithful to answer that kind of prayer. Then we spend the next hour (or sometimes hours) working through forgiveness.

I encourage them to pray, "Lord, I forgive (name) for (what for)" and to go through every remembered pain and abuse. God will bring to their mind many painful memories in order for them to forgive from their heart. He probably has been trying to for years, but they have been suppressing them. One person said, "I can't forgive my mother. I hate her!" "Now you can," I said. God never asks us to lie about how we feel.

He only asks us to let it go from our hearts so He can free us from our past.

I encourage people to stay with the person they are forgiving until every painful memory has surfaced, and then go on to the next person. I have seen experiences surface that they have never talked about or remembered before. Some may respond, "My list is so long, you don't have enough time." I reply, "Yes, I do. I'll stay here all night if I have to." And I mean it. One man started to cry and said, "You're the only person who has ever said that to me."

This type of counseling cannot be done in fifty-minute segments. I am committed to staying with a person through all seven of the Steps to Freedom so he can deal with every area where Satan has had a foothold. Once you start the steps, finish them—don't divide them into separate sessions. A partial resolution gives Satan an opportunity and incentive for increased harassment.

Layers of the Onion

Don't be surprised if people leave feeling free, only to struggle a few weeks or months later. They may conclude it didn't work, but if you check the issues they are dealing with now, they are probably working on another layer of the onion. In many cases, like the stories in this book, the freedom is maintained if they know who they are as children of God and understand the nature of the battle we are in. As long as we are on planet Earth, we will have to pick up our cross daily and follow Jesus. This means putting on the whole armor of God and resisting the world, the flesh and the devil.

In chapter 10, I will be dealing with the issue of severe childhood trauma such as Satanic ritual abuse (SRA). Memories for these people are much more deeply buried. Usually, recall doesn't happen until the victims are in their thirties and forties. The "onion effect" is more pronounced, and always begins with early childhood and works forward. I believe that we are to help these people firmly establish their identity in Christ and then assist them in resolving the conflicts of their past as God slowly reveals it to them.

I have been saying all along that freedom is a prerequisite to growth. You can observe this by the rapid growth that will take place in a person's life when he gains a certain degree of freedom. However, these people will face, as Anne did, many other issues with which they will have to deal. For instance, she felt an oppression come on her one evening, but she had learned that all she had to do to stand against it was what she did—to express verbally the name of Jesus. She was depending on Him to defend her and she was announcing that to the enemy. As other schemes of Satan surface, she is learning to recognize and expose them in the light of the truth, and the truth continues to set her free.

3

Sandy: Freedom From Cultic and Occultic Bondage

When I first met Sandy, she was fleeing from a conference session in fear. She is a pretty lady in her early forties, usually with a bubbly personality and enough energy for two. She has a committed Christian husband, several children, and she lives in a beautiful suburban community.

Sandy had masked very well the battle that had been raging in her mind for most of her life. Few, if any, suspected the war going on inside until she mysteriously started dropping out of her world eighteen months before we met. Here is her story.

* * *

Sandy's Story

*I lived mostly in a very tiny corner
of my mind.*

At last I am able to believe I am a child of God. I am now sure of my place in my Father's heart. He loves me. My spirit bears witness with His Spirit that it is so. I no longer feel outside the family of God—I no longer feel like an orphan.

Since the time we spent together at the conference, the evil presence inside of me is gone, and the many voices that haunted me for thirty-five years are also gone. It feels clean, spacious and beautiful inside *all* of my mind.

Before I found my freedom in Christ, I lived mostly in a very tiny corner of my mind. Even then I could never escape the commanding voices or the filthy language or the accusing anger. So I tried to separate myself from my mind altogether and live a life disassociated from it.

I became a Christian in 1979 and have struggled continually to believe that God actually accepted me, wanted me, cared about me. At last this lifelong struggle has come to an end. Before, I could never hear that still, small voice of God in my mind without being punished for it by the other voices. Today only the still, small voice is there.

I hoped that my father was correct and
that there wasn't any God.

It all started when I was very young. My father professed to be an atheist and my mother was very religious, so there was a lot of conflict and confusion in our home. I went to religious schools, but when I came home I heard from my father that religion was all a lot of nonsense for weak people. I actually hoped that he was correct and that there wasn't any God because I was afraid of my mother's religion. I was afraid that God would get me if I didn't behave correctly. But I was looking for spiritual answers, even though I rejected both of my parents' solutions.

I would communicate with the ball,
using it as a fortune-telling device and
believing that it was magic.

My family, both parents and grandparents, was riddled with superstitious beliefs and good luck charms. I remember visiting my grandparents on my mother's side and feeling that their house was a quiet place to get away from the chaos of the home I was growing up in. She didn't have any toys for me to play with, only a black Crazy 8 ball. There was a window in the ball and little chips inside with probably a hundred different answers. I would ask the ball a question like "Will it rain tomorrow?" And one of the answers would float up to the top such as "Probably."

I grew very attached to that ball and spent a lot of time at my grandmother's house playing with it and believing that it had magic power and answers for everything in my life. I would communicate with the ball about my parents and what was happening in my life, using it as a fortune-telling device. Over a period of time, I saw that many of the answers the ball gave me were correct, confirming my belief that the ball had power.

I suppose the grown-ups thought it was just a toy for the grandchildren to play with. When I had problems, though, I would store them up until I got to my grand-mother's house and try to solve them with the magic ball.

When I visited my father's parents, they would take me to their very legalistic church and I became terrified of hell. Being fearful of God and religion, I turned to the magic ball to try predicting events. That way I could be prepared in advance for any disasters God was going to send my way.

I would become explosively angry over anything. At the same time, I felt like a lonely, sad, scared little girl.

By the time I was fourteen I had become very religious in the Catholic church where, for some reason, I felt safe. While at home, my dad's alcoholism and my parents' fighting intensified and there was no peace. My parents would probably say that I was the problem, that I was a problem child. My mother tried to keep my father and me separated because he was very abusive and I was not passive. I loved to fight and I would always get in between him and anyone he was angry with. He would throw me out of the house whenever he saw me, so eventually I only came home when he was away or asleep.

I was angry and rebellious and hated everyone in authority to the extent that people would walk carefully around me because of my explosive anger. What they didn't know was that inside I felt like a sad, lonely, scared little girl. I just wanted someone to take care of me, but I could never share this. When someone attempted to get close to me, I hid my insecurity by becoming argumentative.

I was a problem at school and in the community, and I became sexually promiscuous—basically doing anything I could that would break the Ten Commandments. Once I went into a Catholic church, looked at the crucifix and said, "Everything You hate, I love; and everything You love, I hate." I was daring God to strike me, and I wasn't even afraid that He might.

---

*I just wanted to be in a family
and be safe.*

At nineteen, I went to a major city and lived with two other girls for two years. In a bar at 2 A.M., a bartender gave us a small calling card and asked, "Why don't you girls go to my church? Maybe you'll find answers to some of your problems and won't have to be out here in the middle of the night." I felt that I might as well try the "church" one more time, believing that all churches were the same. I just wanted to be in a family and feel safe, so the next day we went to that church. I had no idea it was a cult . . . and for ten years, I was involved in it!

Initially, I felt loved; it was my "family." They took an interest in my life. No one had paid that much attention to me before. No one had taken enough notice of me to say, "We want you to get nine hours of sleep. We want you to eat three meals a day. We want to know where you are." They held me accountable for my lifestyle and I interpreted their interest in me as love and concern for my well-being. I would have died for them.

I accepted their philosophy that we are all gods. This

fit in with my father's atheistic views that there really is no supreme God and that religion is just somebody's invention to control people. They also explained who Jesus Christ was and to me that seemed to satisfy my mother's religion. They said that He was just a good teacher like Mohammed or Buddha, but that He wasn't supreme or God, or else He could have prevented Himself from having to die on the cross.

My whole world revolved around the cult's teachings.

The more I got involved, the more the cult consumed my life. I believed everything they said and that anything I read in the newspapers or heard on TV was a lie. So I read nothing unless the cult wrote it, and I believed nothing unless their signature was on it. My whole world revolved around its teaching.

I went through a lot of personal instruction where they told me what to do to become a "totally free spiritual being." Because they taught reincarnation, I believed that I had hundreds of past lifetimes. I "learned" previous names, how many children I had, even the color of my hair. This included lives on other planets. Because I trusted them, I believed them; the reason no one else knew this "truth" about themselves is because they weren't willing to know the truth.

I lived in two worlds.

I tried to live in two worlds. Ever since I was seven years old I have heard voices in my head and had invisible friends. I would live in one world at school but in another world at home. The voices in my head continued speaking to me. The cult leaders said the voices were from my past lifetimes. My ill-fated hope was that they would be put to rest and not bother me anymore when I was fully instructed.

While this was happening, my family moved to

another state and my mother was invited to a neighbor-hood Bible study where she became a born-again Christian. She didn't tell anyone because my father was still an atheist and wouldn't have let her go to the study. But she asked her friends to pray for the conversion of her husband and her kids. Had I known they were praying for me, I, too, would have tried to stop her.

I went to visit my mother on her deathbed with the idea from a cult member to try to convert her.

When my mother became ill with cancer, I visited her on her deathbed with the idea from a cult member to convert her so that we could have her spirit to care for in the next lifetime. In the next lifetime, she would live in the cult and I could become aware of her. Then she would have a better life than the one she had with dad.

While visiting her, I felt total hatred for her friends who came into her room and talked about Jesus and prayed for her healing. I ridiculed their attempts, but was astounded by the strength of my mother's convictions. It was a battle between her mind and mine, but one night she was in so much pain, and so worn down emotionally, that she went through a commitment prayer with me to give her spirit to my cult. Satisfied, I went home the next day, and she died several days later.

I remember playing Scrabble with a neighbor at three o'clock one afternoon when suddenly I sensed the presence of my mother in the room. I said, "What are you doing here? You should go to headquarters where you are supposed to be." Later that day, my brother called and told me that my mother had died around that time in the afternoon.

My friend in the cult told me that everything was fine—they had received my mother's spirit. Eventually they would call me when the baby was born who would receive my mother's spirit, so that I could go to see this baby.

> *That made me so angry that I stole*
> *a Bible to highlight all of the lies.*

About a week later, I received a letter from one of my mother's friends who had been with her when she died. She said that my mother had gone to be with Jesus. That made me so angry that I went to a local church and stole a Bible. I was going to highlight all of the lies and then send it to this lady to show her how confused she was and to convert her to the cult.

I opened the Bible to the middle and began reading in the book of Isaiah. Instead of highlighting the "lies," I found myself highlighting words like "Come let us reason together says the Lord . . . If you will turn to Me, I will turn to you." I discovered the book is filled with passages about not getting involved with mediums and astrologers. By the time I was finished, I was confused about what the truth was.

I had never read a Bible before, much less owned one, so I turned to the back to see how it ended. When I read the Book of Revelation, I was scared because the cult teaches the Book of Revelation backwards. They say that people are really "gods" who go back and take their rightful place in heaven.

> *I sat there trying to get in touch*
> *with my mother's spirit.*

I went to the church where I stole the Bible and tried to get in touch with my mother's spirit. I figured that if she was a Christian, then I should be able to go to a Christian place and contact her. When I got to the church, a middle-aged couple approached me and asked if they could help me in any way. When I told them I was trying to get in touch with my mother, they lovingly said that they didn't think I would find her there, but they invited me to have breakfast with them and talk about it. It turned out to be a Christian Fellowship Breakfast where, for the first time in my life, I was with a group of people whose lives seemed special because of their relationship to Jesus Christ.

The next several months my confusion continued as I went back and forth between reading my Bible and my cult books. I visited the church where I had met the couple, and they would come over to my house just to read Scripture with me. I consider them my spiritual mother and father. They never made me feel evil or bad; they just loved and accepted me. Every month they would pick me up and take me to their Christian breakfast and other church services.

But if she had really gone to be with Jesus, then I wanted to be there too.

During this time I remember praying and telling God that wherever my mother went is where I wanted to be. If I caused her to lose heaven because of what I did, then I didn't want to be a Christian. I wanted to be with her. But if she had really gone to be with Jesus, as her friend who wrote me said, then I wanted to be there too. I just couldn't choose.

One night I had a dream where I saw my mother walking toward me with another person in white, and she said, "I forgive you for what you did and I want you to forgive yourself and to pray for your father." That woke me like a shot. I awakened my husband and said, "I know where she is." I was angry that she had asked me to pray for my father, but that's how I know it was my mother. No one else would dare ask me to do that.[1]

The next week I went to church with that couple, gave my life to the Lord and renounced my cult involvement. I gave them all of my cult books and paraphernalia and they took it out of the house. For the next two years I was discipled by them and their fellowship group.

---

1. In the parable of the rich man and Lazarus, we are clearly told of the great chasm that separates the living from the dead. I do not believe it was actually Sandy's mother who appeared in her dream. There is no way to know for sure, but perhaps God used Sandy's sensitivity toward her mother as a means of communicating with her and drawing her to Himself.

Six weeks after becoming a Christian I found out that I was pregnant. I was angry with the Lord. I had already had three abortions and decided that I shouldn't have to go through with the pregnancy just because I was a Christian. But my husband said, "I thought you were a Christian and that Christians don't believe in abortions." It angered me that God would speak to me through my husband who wasn't even a Christian, but God seemed to say to me, "Listen, your home is big enough for a baby, how about your heart? Is it big enough?" That's when I decided to keep the baby.

Nine months after the baby was born my husband gave his life to the Lord. He said, "When you decided against an abortion, I was impressed by God's intervention and impact in your life."

A priest learned of my background and suggested that I probably needed deliverance.

I wondered if I should become a Catholic as my mother had been. My spiritual parents said it would be all right to go to the Catholic church, so I went to a charismatic Catholic prayer group. When the priest learned of my background he suggested that I probably needed deliverance, so I met with him. He started talking to whatever was inside of me, asking its name. The "thing" would give him a name and become angry and violent; I became frightened and beat up the priest.

It scared me so much I decided to keep all of this a secret. I wanted to believe that if I were really a Christian, God would make that horrible presence go away. Because it didn't, I couldn't believe I had a relationship with God. People would tell me I was saved since I had given my heart to the Lord, but no one could provide the assurance I was looking for. I felt half evil and half good, and I couldn't see how half of me could go to heaven.

I would go to church, but when I came
home the voices tormented me.
They were no longer my friends.

We moved again, had more children, and got involved in a new church and Bible studies. I still had this separated life. I would go to church, but when I came home the voices tormented me. They were no longer my friends. They were accusing, screaming, angry and profane. They told me, "You think that you're a Christian, but you're not. You're dirty and sinful." And the more involved I became as a Christian, the worse the voices became.

I became legalistic, thinking that I had to go to every Bible study and church activity. I went Sunday morning and Sunday and Wednesday evenings, feeling that being present every time the church was open was the only way I could prove that I was a Christian.

I went on mission trips and taught Sunday school. When I taught Bible studies and shared the dangers of cults with others, everything inside me became intensified. Anger became rage, the pain became torment, the accusations made me feel suicidal. I thought, *Why don't I just kill myself? I can't ever be good enough to be a real Christian.*

When I went on a radio program and talked about the dangers of cults, I was plagued with fear that my kids would be killed. I became paranoid about even sending them to school so I dropped everything. When I withdrew, I temporarily felt better and the voices lessened, but I became a loner—not going anywhere or talking to anybody, just wanting to be by myself all the time. I felt more and more bound, and my internal life became a prison where no light could shine.

I was diagnosed as MPD
(multiple personality disorder).

I went to Christian counseling and it did help me to sort out my abusive childhood and put some things together. I was diagnosed as having a dissociative disorder because of the voices and MPD (multiple personality disorder), because many times I would say, "Well, we feel this way." My counselor would ask, "Why are you saying 'we'?" I would say, "I don't know."

This frightened me, but I was also relieved to know that someone believed there were voices inside me. I went to counseling two days a week trying to relieve the pain and the torment. If at any time there was an apparent look in the right direction, I was fearful, and then I felt the need to punish myself by doing anything dangerous or painful. Nothing quieted the rage inside me but worship and praise tapes. Only while listening to them did I feel that I wasn't going crazy, but I could only listen, never sing.

The counselors loved me and were faithfully there for me every week. They prayed for me and promised to stay with me for the journey. They felt it would take a long time for me to become integrated. They gave me hope, assuring me that God wanted me to be whole and that He would bring it about. I vacillated between hope and despair like I was on a roller coaster. The Christian counselors were a lifeline for me. I felt God's love and acceptance through their listening, understanding and caring.

However, when I was seven a traumatic event had occurred in my life which resulted in such tremendous fear that even in counseling I could never progress beyond that point. I would get to the age of seven and then be too afraid to go on. I reasoned, *If it's that bad, I don't want to know what it is.* A voice in my head told me that I would be harmed if I remembered.

My neighbor was my friend and knew about my struggle. One day she asked me if I would help her prepare for a "Resolving Personal and Spiritual Conflicts Conference" that was coming to her church in about six weeks—visiting churches, putting up posters and selling the books. I didn't want to do it. I was sure the conference was just one more meeting like the ones I had already tried. Every time I had come home so lonely and discouraged, knowing my punishment waited for me for even trying to find a cure. I was afraid it would make my life more miserable, but I half-heartedly said that I would help.

After watching ten minutes of the first video, I decided that I hated Neil Anderson.

My neighbor gave me videos of the conference to preview so that I would be able to answer questions about the materials. After watching only ten minutes of the first video, I decided that I hated Neil Anderson and that he didn't have anything to say. I felt like telling people not to go and said to my neighbor, "I don't like him. Are you sure you want him to come and give this conference? I think there's something wrong with him." She replied, "Well, you're the only one who has told me that and I've talked to about thirty-five people."

At the conference, my resistance increased and I didn't hear all of what was said. I couldn't remember the nights Neil talked about our identity in Christ, and I sat in the second row unable to sing any of the hymns. He would speak and a part of me would say, *That's not new. We all knew that anyway.* Another little voice inside of me would say, *I sure wish that everything he said is true and that this man could help me.* But I never revealed that hopeful part, only my critical part. Talking with others I would say, "So what do you think of the conference? It's really not that great, is it?"

I started choking, felt sick and headed for my car to go home.

Near the end of the week a two-hour taped counseling session was shown. I could not watch the woman on the video finding her freedom. I felt fear and anger all at the same time. I started choking, felt sick and headed for my car to go home, determined not to show up again on Saturday. But Neil was in the hallway between me and my car.

We went into a side room and Neil walked me through some renunciations where I verbally repeated a series of statements, taking a stand against Satan and all of his influences in my life. I also prayed that God would reveal to me whatever it was that prevented me from sitting to watch the video, and that's when I remembered what happened when I was seven years old. It was like the clouds rolled away and I saw myself as a little girl, terrified of a dark, black presence.

I was playing with dolls in the back bedroom of our home. It was daytime and nothing frightening was happening and no one else was present in the room. But suddenly I felt total fear. I remember stopping my play and laying down, facing the ceiling and saying, "What do you want?" to a huge, black presence that was over me. The presence said to me, "Can I share your body with you?" And I said, "If you promise not to kill me, you can."

I actually felt that presence totally infiltrating me from head to toe. It was so oppressive to have this thing go into every pore of my body that I remember thinking, *I am going to die.* I was only seven, but it was so sexual and so dirty that I felt I had a big secret I had to hide and that I could never tell anyone. From that time on I felt that I had more than one personality, and it seemed natural to share my body with unseen others. Sometimes I would do things and not remember them when people would tell me. And I would think, *Well that wasn't me. That was my invisible 'friend' who did that.*

I never played with the black ball again. I only spoke with my invisible friend who would suggest things that I should do. Sometimes the suggestions were bad, but sometimes they were good. Because I needed companionship in my abusive childhood, I never thought the voice was anything other than a friend.

Whenever I would tell him, Neil would say, "That's a lie." And he gently went through the Steps to Freedom.

As Neil led me by giving me the words to speak, I specifically renounced all Satanic guardians that had been assigned to me. At that point I was startled by the presence of evil and afraid we would both be beaten up. It reminded me that I had played with that magic ball for years.

Neil told me not to be afraid and asked what the presence was saying to my mind. Whenever I told him what the voices were saying, he would say, "That's a lie," and he gently led me through the Steps to Freedom. I can remember the very second the presence wasn't there anymore. I felt like the small, little person that was really me was being blown up like a balloon inside of me. Finally, after thirty-five years of fractured living, I was the only person inside. The place that evil presence vacated I have now dedicated to my new occupant: the clean, gentle, quiet spirit of God.

Saturday morning I was afraid to wake up, thinking *This isn't real.* I didn't want to open my eyes because usually the voice would say something like, "Get up, you stupid little slut. You've got work to do." So I would get up and do whatever it said. But that morning there were no voices and I laid in my bed thinking, *There's no one here but me.*

When I went back to the conference and walked in the door, people noticed that I looked different. I told them how I had always felt like an orphan in the body of Christ, but now I felt free and part of the family of God.

I became convinced that God wanted it gone as much as I did.

I thought that as soon as Neil left, this thing was going to come back. But the peace lasted, because Jesus Christ is the one who set me free. Whenever that fear would come I would go through the Steps to Freedom by myself, something I did at least four or five more times. I became convinced that God wanted it gone as much as I did, and it's never been there since.

A week later, we had a head-on car collision. I was afraid the voice would be there to say, "I'm going to crush you because you think you're free." Instead I sensed God saying, "I am here to protect you and I'll always be here like this."

When one of my girls asked me if the wreck was her

fault, I wondered why she felt this way. I remembered that one of the Steps to Freedom is breaking the ancestral ties because demonic strongholds can be passed on from one generation to the next (Exodus 20:4,5). As we talked, my ten-year-old told me, "Sometimes I know things are going to happen before they happen. And sometimes I look out the window and see things that nobody else sees."

Instantly, I knew that my daughter also needed to be released from bondage. So I took her through the steps, paraphrasing the big words into her language. She prayed to cancel out all demonic working that was passed on from her ancestors, rejecting any way in which Satan might be claiming ownership of her. She declared herself to be eternally and completely signed over and committed to the Lord Jesus Christ. Since then she has never again experienced that demonic presence.

My husband was away during the conference, and when he came home I told him everything that had happened. The next Sunday, in our Sunday school class, the leader asked if anyone wanted to share about the conference. My husband stood and said, "I want to share even though I wasn't there, because the Lord gave me a new wife to come home to."

---

*Now I feel God's face toward me
and sense His smile.*

Before, I didn't have a self-image. Every day I felt that God had a measure of mercy for me and that some day it would run out, that even God Himself must wonder why He made me. I just knew that someday He was going to say, "I've had enough of Sandy." So every day I would pray, "God, please don't let it be today. Let me get this one last thing done before You do it."

It was so freeing when Neil taught that God and Satan are not co-equal, but that God is off the charts and Satan is way beneath Him, that we should not make the mistake of thinking he has divine attributes. I had always thought that God and Satan were co-equal, fighting it out for us, and that God was basically saying, "You can have Sandy."

I had cried to God constantly since my conversion:

Create a clean heart in me!
Renew a right spirit in me!
Please don't cast me out of Your presence!
Please don't take Your Holy Spirit from me!

Over and over I had prayed these prayers for myself, agonizing to know the Lord in a warm and personal way, but feeling like I had a relationship with God's back. Now I feel His face toward me and sense His smile.

Now I don't live in a tiny corner of my mind or outside of my body. I live inside, sharing my mind with only my precious Lord. What a profound difference! There are no words to adequately describe the peacefulness and absence of pain and torment that I now experience daily. It's like being blind all these years and now I see. Everything is new, precious and treasured because it doesn't look black. I'm not afraid anymore that I'll be punished for every move I make. I'm able to make decisions now and have choices. I am free to make mistakes!

The last year and a half I had become unable to have anyone touch me without feeling pain or having horrible sexual thoughts. While having sex I would watch it from outside of my body. When that evil presence claimed to be my "husband" I knew why I had always felt like a prostitute, even as a Christian.

After exposing that lie and renouncing it, I have since come to understand the meaning of "bride" for the first time in my life, after twenty years of marriage, and I now also feel the love from the Bridegroom I shall someday see.

He has wiped away my tears, and answered the cry of my heart. At last, I sense a right Spirit inside of me, and the presence cast out was not the presence of God, but of the evil one. I was fearful that God's presence would leave me. I now feel clean inside. I continue to go to Christian counseling, and I am making progress. I am learning to face and let go of the past abuse. I am learning to live in community and trust others again after feeling betrayed by my cult experience.

I believe God in His loving kindness met me at my point of need, and ordained the meeting that exposed and expelled the Satanic oppression in my life. Now I can continue growing in the family of God. I now am certain I belong to this family, and I'm loved by it. God has shown me that He is faithful and able, not just to call me from darkness to light, but also to keep me and sustain me until the journey ends when I shall see Him face to face. I still face trials, temptations and the pain of living in a fallen world, but I walk in it sensing the strong heartbeat of a loving Father within. The Satanic interference has been removed.

Praise the Lord.

* * *

Parents Must Know Satan's Strategies

The hideousness of Satan is revealed in Sandy's life story. Would he actually take advantage of a child with dysfunctional parents and grandparents who ignorantly provided occultic toys for their grandchildren? Satan would and does.

I have traced the origin of many adult problems to childhood fantasies, imaginary friends, games, the occult and abuses. It is not enough to warn our children about the stranger in the street. What about the one who may appear in their room? Our research indicates that half of our professing Christian teenagers have had some experience in their room that frightened them. That, more than anything, has prompted Steve Russo and me to write *The Seduction of Our Children*. We want to help parents know how to protect their children and defeat the influence of darkness. At the back of that book, I have written some simplified Steps to Freedom for children and early teens.

Truth, Not Power Encounter

In the area of deliverance, the priest's noble but disastrous attempt at an exorcism is one reason why I don't advocate the power encounter approach where the counselor deals directly with the demon. It can be like sticking a broom handle in a hornet's nest, rattling it around and proclaiming, "Hey, there are demons here!" That experience left Sandy terrorized and reluctant to address the issue again. I interacted only with Sandy, not the demons.

The brain is the control center, and as long as Sandy was willing to share with me what was going on inside we never lost control. Accusing and terrorizing thoughts were bombarding her mind. When she revealed what she was hearing, I would simply expose the deception by saying, "That's a lie," or by asking Sandy to renounce it as a lie and tell it to go. The power of Satan is in the lie; when the lie is exposed the power is broken. God's truth sets people free. Occasionally I will have a person ask God to reveal what it is that is keeping him in bondage, and it's not uncommon for past events (often blocked memories) to be brought to mind so the person can confess and renounce them. In Sandy's case, she had no conscious memory of what happened when she was seven. (A biblical means of getting at those memories will be discussed in chapter 10.)

Exercising Authority in Christ

Her concern about my leaving town is another reason I like to deal only with the person. When she asked me what she was going to do when I wasn't there, I responded, "I didn't do anything. You did the renouncing and you exercised your authority in Christ by telling the evil presence to go. Jesus Christ is your deliverer and He will always be with you." She renounced her invitation to let the demon share her body. Later she renounced all her cult and occult experiences. It cannot be overstated how important this step is; it's tied into the whole concept of repentance.

The church throughout its history has publicly declared, "I renounce you Satan and *all* your works and *all* your ways." Most Catholic, orthodox and liturgical churches still make that profession, but for some reason evangelical churches don't. That generic statement needs to be applied specifically for each individual. Any dabbling in the occult, brush with cults or seeking false guidance must be confessed and renounced. *All* his works and *all* his ways need to be renounced as God brings them to our memory. All lies and counterfeit ways must be replaced by "the way and the truth and the life" (John 14:6, NIV).This is done in the first of the Steps to Freedom: Counterfeit versus Real.

Satan's Bondages

Sandy had never had a "normal" sexual relationship. She perceived herself as a prostitute because the evil presence claimed to be her husband. Freedom from that bondage allowed her to have a loving, intimate relationship with her husband. I will have much more to say about sexual bondages after other testimonies.

The mental battle she suffered is quite typical of those in bondage. Most people caught in a spiritual conflict will talk about their dysfunctional family background or other abuses, but seldom will they reveal the battle going on for their minds. They already fear they are going crazy, and they don't relish the thought of it being confirmed. Nor do they like the prospect of prescription drugs.

Sandy was relieved when her Christian counselor believed her. The secular world has no other alternative than to look for a physical cure, since mental illness is the only possible diagnosis. The tragedy of anti-psychotic medications, when the problem is actually spiritual, is the drugged state in which it leaves the recipient. How is the truth going to set someone free who is so medicated that he or she can hardly talk, much less think?

Christian counselors with whom I have dialogued are greatly appreciative of being made aware of spiritual conflict and how to resolve it. This makes their counseling practice much more wholistic and effective.

One lady shared in the middle of a conference that I was describing her to a "T." She said she was going to a treatment center for thirty days. I asked if I could see her first since I knew that the treatment center she was going to was notorious in its use of drugs for therapy. She agreed and wrote the following:

After meeting with you Monday night, I was absolutely

euphoric, and so was my husband. He was so happy to see me happy. I was finally able to take my position with Christ and renounce the deceiver. The Lord has released me from my bondage.

My big news is that I didn't wake up with nightmares or screams. Instead I woke up with my heart singing! The very first thought that entered my mind was "even the stones will cry out" followed by "Abba Father." Neil, the Holy Spirit is alive in me! Praise the Lord! I can't begin to tell you how free I feel, but somehow I think you know!

Assuming Responsibility

Nightmares and voices may have a spiritual explanation for their origin and the church bears the responsibility to check it out. I believe that every pastor and Christian counselor should be able to help people like this.

You have nothing to lose by going through or taking someone through the Steps to Freedom. It's just old-fashioned house cleaning which takes into account the reality of the spiritual world. All we are doing is helping people assume responsibility for their relationship with God. Nobody is accusing anybody of anything. If there is nothing demonic going on in someone's life, the worst thing that can happen is that the person will really be ready for communion the next time it is served!

Sandy's story brings out very well the two most sought-after goals we have with this type of counseling. First, that people will know who they are as children of God, that they are a part of God's forever family. Second, that they will have a peace and quietness in their mind, the peace that guards our hearts and our minds, the peace which transcends all understanding (Philippians 4:7).

4

Jennifer:
Freedom From
Eating Disorders

I received a call from Jennifer asking if I would spend some time with her if she flew out. I set aside one Monday morning and had the privilege to walk her through the Steps to Freedom. A month later I received the following letter.

Dear Neil,

I just wanted to write and thank you for the time you spent with me. I guess I felt like nothing happened at the time we prayed and that maybe there wasn't a problem with the demonic. I was wrong. Something really did happen, and I have not had one more self-destructive thought or action or compulsion since that day.

I think the deliverance process began through my prayers of repentance in the months following my suicide attempt. I don't understand it all, but I know something is really different in my life and I feel free today. I haven't cut myself in a month and that is a true miracle.

I have a few questions I wish you would respond to if you have time. They have to do with my psychological problems. I was told that I have a chronic manic-depressive, schizo-affective disorder, and I am on Lithium and an anti-psychotic medication. Do I need these? Am I really chronic?

I always felt during my acting out periods, which is what they based my diagnosis on, that it was not me but rather some strong power outside myself that drove me to act self-destructive and crazy. The last three times I have quit my Lithium I have become suicidal and ended up in the hospital. I don't want that to happen again, but was that demonic? I also had a lot of mood swings even on the pills, but since my visit with you I have had none! This makes me wonder if I'm really okay and don't need the pills.

Also, ever since I was a little girl I have never been able to pray; there always seemed to be a wall between me and God. I was never very happy and always felt a sense of fear and uneasiness, like something was wrong.

Jennifer

Jennifer's story is important because it clarifies the need to know who we are as children of God and the nature of the spiritual battle we are in. That one morning we were able to process a lot, and she did achieve a sense of freedom. But does she know who she is as a child of God, and does she know how to stay free in Christ?

Within six months Jennifer was having difficulty again. Another year passed before she was desperate enough to call. She decided to fly out again, but this time she attended a whole conference. Here is her story.

*   *   *

Jennifer's Story

Everything seemed like a dream and everybody was just a character.

In seventh grade my eating disorder started—overeating, then starving. I would babysit and clean out the refrigerator, and then I wouldn't eat anything for three or four days. My focus became my weight; I was obsessed with the need to be thin.

Everything around me seemed like a dream and everybody was just a character. I thought, *Someday I will wake up, but I won't know the dreamer.* Nothing seemed real. I lived in a "checked-out" state. I didn't think. When people talked I would look at them in bewilderment because I wasn't in touch with my mind.

During the day I appeared normal and functioned fairly well in school. Nighttimes were weird with a lot of bad dreams and terror. I wept often because of the voices in my head and the images and nonsense thoughts that often filled my mind. But I never said a word to anyone. I knew people would think I was crazy and I was terrified that nobody would believe me.

My college years were really hard, filled with routine binging and purging. I lost thirty pounds and began fainting and having chest pains. Because I was pathetically thin from anorexia, the skin literally hung on my bones. Finally I agreed to be hospitalized. I was totally exhausted physically, mentally and spiritually.

I nearly died. My pulse was forty when I was admitted, and they had trouble finding my blood pressure. My parents were very supportive. The hospital was good and I had Christian therapists, but they never touched on the spiritual. I was cutting myself, using razor blades and knives, and I still have scars on my hands from digging holes into them with my fingernails.

---

*I crawled down the hall,
trying to get away from the things
flying around my room.*

The voices and nighttimes were bad, with demonic visitations and something raping me at night, holding me down so I couldn't move. Sometimes I crawled down the hall, trying to get away from things flying around my room. I was terrorized; thoughts of cutting my heart out dominated my mind. I did actually cut on my chest with knives because I thought my heart was poison and that I needed to get rid of it so that I would be clean.

When childhood memories started to surface, I lost it. I was back in the hospital again and absolutely out of control. On some days it required five or six people to restrain me. I would be out of my body watching those people hold me down while I was fighting and kicking, until they would sedate me. I was diagnosed as manic-depressive. I took Lithium and continued with anti-depressants for the next six years and the drugs did quiet me somewhat.

While I was in the hospital a friend suggested that I talk with Neil Anderson, but I told her no. The thought of there being something demonic was terrifying to me and I told her, "God said if two or more people pray He would listen. Why can't several people just pray with me here in the hospital? Why do I have to have some man come?" I talked with my Christian counselors and they said, "Your associates just want to make this spiritual because they don't want to deal with the pain in your life." The counselors had gained my trust that year, so I believed them and refused to see Neil. That's the first time I ever heard Neil's name. I did not meet him for three years. I was too afraid; the whole idea freaked me out.

I would do a fantastic job at work,
then get in my car and pull out
my razor blades.

Somehow, I graduated and started working. I would do a fantastic job at work, then get in my car, pull out my razor blades and live in a different world for the next sixteen hours. Then I would go back to work. I was talking with all of my "friends" in my head and cutting ritualistically on myself for the blood. I just wanted to feel; I knew I was not in touch with reality.

At night I would often lie awake, hoping I would die before morning. I wrote suicide notes and knew every empty house around: houses that were for sale, where I could drive my car into the garage, leave the motor running and kill myself. I also knew the gun shops in town and their hours, so that if I needed a gun I could get one. I kept two or three hundred pills at home so I always had an "out" for when I could bare it no longer. I had many plans to commit suicide.

I prayed to God that I could get through one more night.

I kept thinking, *The Lord has got to get me through this.* I knew He was my only hope and that there was a reason to live, so I kept crying out to Him. I remember crawling into a corner of my room at night and sleeping there on the floor. I was trying to get away from it all and praying to God that I could get through one more night. I prayed that He would give me strength and protect me from myself. I blamed myself for all of this.

I feared for my life and so did many of my friends. I went to see a pastor and told him I thought I had a spiritual problem and that I also felt I was going to die. He said, "You have one of the best psychiatrists in town; I don't know why you're talking to me." Then he asked, "Are you taking your medicine?" He was scared of me and he didn't know how to help me.

Once I spent several hours talking with some caring friends. One suggested, "Jennifer, you just need to go into the throne room of Jesus." The voices inside me said, "That's it!" To me, "going into the throne room" meant to die. I drove to a hotel, went to a room and took two hundred pills. I laid down by my simple note that read, *I'm going home to be with Jesus. I just can't take it anymore.*

I didn't want to be alone when I died.

I called someone because I didn't want to be alone when I died. I felt that if there was someone on the other end of the phone it would help. At first I wouldn't give the phone number to my friend, but later I was so sleepy and out of it that I gave in so I could go to sleep and my friend could call me back later. Two-and-a-half hours later they found me and took me to a hospital where my stomach was pumped. I was placed in the intensive care unit. I should have died, but by a miracle of God I didn't.

I was hospitalized again in a different Christian clinic. The possibility of my problem being spiritual was never addressed. I was diagnosed as being schizo-affective and bi-polar. They told me I didn't know reality and that I needed to base my confidence on what others said and not on what was going on in my head. They told me I would be dependent on medication for the rest of my life. The side effects of the anti-psychotics and anti-depressants were horrendous. The tremors were so bad that I had trouble even using my hand to write my name, and my vision was blurred. I was so drugged I couldn't even hold my mouth open.

They never explored the possibility of the demonic.

In counseling I told them I was hearing voices, but they never explored the possibility of them being demonic. They did tell me that since I had a lot of therapy already, they wanted to deal with me on the spiritual level. They brought in a godly man who was good, but I couldn't hear or remember a word he said. As soon as he opened his Bible and started to talk, I began listening to other things and planning to kill myself. I felt that if I could just get out of there I would do it, and this time I would be successful.

One day a friend called me at the clinic and honestly addressed the sin in my life. He basically told me I was being manipulative, dishonest, hateful, attention-seeking and selfish. That was heavy stuff, but he spoke kindly and I was at a point where I was ready to hear it. I got on my knees and wrote a letter to God in my journal asking forgiveness. Those sins were a part of me that I was ashamed of and I had lived with the guilt of them all my life. I did experience some release and I know that was the beginning of my healing.

The voices were talking so loud I couldn't hear a word he said.

Friends invited me to California for a visit, and I decided I wanted to meet Neil Anderson. I went to his office and we talked for about two hours. He opened his Bible and was going through the Scriptures, but the voices were so loud I couldn't hear a word he said. It was like he was talking gibberish—his words were like another language. That's how it always was with me when people were using the Bible.

I got through the Steps to Freedom, but I didn't feel any different when I left. I wondered if the words just went straight from my eyes to my mouth without my internalizing anything I was reading. But then two areas improved. The struggle with food was better, and I never cut myself again. The voices were also gone for a couple of weeks, but then they came back. I didn't remember Neil saying what to do when the voices and thoughts came back, and it never occurred to me that I didn't have to listen. I didn't know I had a choice, so I got hit worse than ever.

Six months later I was in the hospital again, both suicidal and psychotic. I was out of it and did everything the voices were telling me to do. I was encouraged to see Neil again, but if that didn't work I knew I was going to die. All of this had been going on for seven terrible years, and the side effects of the drugs were so bad that all I did was work four hours and then sit in front of the TV or sleep. I couldn't carry on a meaningful conversation with anybody, and I really didn't care about anything anymore. I felt hopeless, exhausted and discouraged.

I went to the conference on Resolving Personal and Spiritual Conflicts. I again met with Neil and at one point I got so sick that I threw up. He introduced me to a lady with a past similar to mine. She sat beside me and prayed for me, so I was more able to hear and comprehend what Neil was saying.

I learned a lot about the spiritual battle that was going on for my mind and what I needed to do to take a stand. Once that part became clear, I was free. I knew what to do and how to do it. Previously, I didn't know how to stay free and walk in my freedom, although I was raised in a good Christian home. Even though I accepted Christ when I was four, I never knew who I was in Christ and I didn't understand the authority I had as a child of God.

My psychiatrist would not support me in going off my medication.

I told my psychiatrist that I was free in Christ now and wanted to get off my medication. He said, "You've tried this before and look at your history." I said, "But it's different now. Will you support me in this?" When he said "No, I can't," I replied, "Well I'm going to do it anyway; I'll take responsibility for myself."

He said he would see me in a month. I came back in a month and was functioning on half of the prescription, and in two months I was off completely. He asked how I felt and when I told him I was fine, he shook my hand and said I wouldn't need to come back anymore. It was like I was discovering life for the first time, and I felt impressed to write the following letter to Neil:

Dear Neil:

I was reading back over my journals from years past and was harshly reminded of the darkness and evil in which I was engulfed for so many years. I often wrote about "them" and the control they had of me. I often felt that rather than be torn between Satan and God, I would rather rest in the darkness. What I did not realize was that I was a child of God and *in* Christ, not hanging between two spirits. So often I felt that I was being controlled and was crazy, having lost all sense of self and reality. I think in a way I had learned to like the darkness. I felt safe there and was deceived by the lie that if I let go of the evil, I would die and God would not meet my needs or care for me the way I wanted.

This is why I would not talk with you the first time. I didn't want you to take away the only thing I had, feeling sheer terror at the thought. I guess the evil one had something to do with those thoughts and fears. I was so deceived. I really tried to pray and read the Bible, but it all made little sense. Once I tried to read *The Adversary* by Mark Bubeck, and I literally could not make my hand pick it up. I just stared at it.

Psychiatrists tried many different medications and doses (including large doses of anti-psychotics) to make things better. I took up to fifteen pills a day just to remain in control and somewhat functional. I was so drugged I couldn't think or feel much at all. I felt like a walking dead person! The therapists and doctors all agreed I had a chronic mental illness that I would deal with for the rest of my life—a very defeating prognosis to hear!

At the conference, I saw the total picture. Just weeks before I had made the decision that I did not want to entertain the darkness any longer and that I really wanted to get well, but I had no idea how to take that step. Well . . . I learned, and once again my head became quiet. The voices stopped, the doubts and confusion lifted, and I was free. Now I know how to stand.

I feel like a small child who has been through a horrible and terrifying storm, lost in confusion and loneliness. I knew my loving Father was on the other side of the door and that He was my only hope and relief, but I could not get through that strong door. Then someone told me how to turn the knob and told me that because I was God's child, I had all the authority and right to open the door. I have reached up and opened the door and run to my Father and now I am resting in His safe and loving arms. I know and believe that "neither death, nor life, neither angels, nor principalities, neither things present nor things to come, nor any powers, nor height, nor depth, nor any created thing, shall be able to separate us from the love of God" (Romans 8:38).

Now I feel peaceful and full inside.

I am working in ministry now, taking tons of time to read and pray and be loved by the God I had heard so much about but never experienced. I am giving and sharing and serving in ways I have always dreamed of doing. In bondage, I could never reach beyond my desperate self. Now I feel peaceful and full inside, somewhat childlike, with purpose and direction, joy and hope.

Now when I get accusing or negative thoughts, they just bounce off because I have learned to bind Satan with one quick sentence, ignore his lies and choose the truth. It works! Because of my strong Savior, Satan leaves me alone almost instantly. I've had a few pretty down days, but then I choose to remember who I am and tell Satan and his demons to leave. It's a miracle . . . the cloud lifts!

My sadness has come when I realize I have lived most of my life in captivity, believing lies. I try to remember, "For this purpose I have raised you up, that I may show My power in you, and that My name may be declared in all the earth" (Exodus 9:16, NKJV). I know God will use my experiences mightily in my own life as well as in others. The chains have fallen off. I have chosen the light and life.

Because of the obvious changes in my countenance, people have been seeking me out for light and truth. I can't keep up with "who has which" of your tapes. I have shared them a lot with others who find themselves in bondage and need.

---

*I needed to see that the sick person
is not who I am.*

I am still seeing a Christian counselor and this has been very helpful. It's horrendous coming out of my past, and it's a struggle learning how to live. My biggest temptation is to be sick because I got a lot of strokes from that. I needed to see that the sick person is not who I am, but that I am a child of God and that He desires for me to be free. It was difficult for me to accept that new identity. A few times I have had "crazy" days. But I realize that this is not what I want, and I call my friend to pray with me and renounce the darkness with her encouragement.

My biggest fight is to stay single-minded because

my tendency is to let my mind split off. My prayer every day is that He will help me to stay focused and that I will love Him with all my heart and soul, not just a part of it.

Another important friend is a woman who was delivered five years ago from being a medium in New Age. She has been a tremendous help, but my main support is the friend I met at your conference. Our phone bills are huge and we see each other three or four times a year. I really don't think I would have made it and stayed free those first couple of months without her.

My family did everything they knew to love me.

My family and the treatment I received were the best. They did everything they knew to love me, help me and save my life. I have been so loved throughout my life by so many friends and family members. I feel it is because of their prayers, consistent love and support that I am alive today.

I firmly believe that the prescription drugs were what kept me from being able to think or fight. They left me in such a passive, semi-alert state that I couldn't concentrate. I couldn't write because of horrible hand tremors . . . I couldn't see at times because of blurred vision . . . I couldn't pray because there was no concentration . . . and never did I have the energy to discern thoughts or remember truths in Scripture . . . and I couldn't follow conversation. It was like being on twelve to fifteen antihistamine tablets at one time, leaving me in a very helpless condition, with no quality of life.

I pull out my cards and read them aloud until the light dispels the darkness.

I have written out a ton of truth verses on cards

that I carry everywhere. There have been times when
the dark cloud of oppression is so crushing. That's
when I pull out my cards and read them aloud until
the light dispels the darkness and I'm able to pray
again. Then I can find the lie I've been believing, claim
the truth, announce my position in Christ and
renounce the devil. The process has become so routine
that I find myself claiming and renouncing under my
breath, almost without thinking.

My friend and I have talked often of an active
surrender. How do I acknowledge my total dependence upon God and fight at the same time? I don't
totally understand it, but it is an active surrender that
sets us free.

My most difficult struggle to this day is to want to
be free. I'm tempted to use my dissociative "alters" or
friends. They occupied the places in my split-off self
where I used to go to escape reality and find relief.
Satan takes advantage of those mental escapes, playing havoc in my mind and life.

I now desire to find my safety in God.

I actually buried stones in the ground representing
each split-off piece of my mind that I had held on to.
In one sense, it was a huge loss. In another, I knew I
had to do that because those identities and psychotic-
like splits were homes where Satan and his workers
resided. I still am tempted, and even have returned to
those states when I am under stress, but I fight it and
I am able to bounce back. I'm grasping for God's love
and strength in a way I'd never been able to before. I
now desire to find my safety in Him.

I cannot express the difference in my heart and
life. Where my heart used to reside in pieces, now it
is whole. Where my mind was void, now there is a song
and an intellect beyond anything I could have previously comprehended. Where there was a life of
unreality and despair, now there is joy and freedom
and light. To God be the glory because all I have done

is to finally say "yes" to His offer of freedom. I am grateful to be alive!

Jennifer

*   *   *

Getting and Staying Free

When Jennifer saw me the first time, I led her through the Steps to Freedom. The fact that there was some resolution was clear from the first letter she sent. However, in a short, three-hour counseling session neither I nor anyone else have enough time to educate sufficiently regarding identity in Christ, much less the nature of the spiritual battle. Plus, I didn't have the experience base then that I do now. Since Jennifer lacked this knowledge, she slipped back into her old habit patterns. In her second visit, she sat through a whole conference designed to give her the information she needed to get and stay free.

Most pastors can't afford the time to sit one-on-one with people for extended teaching sessions. I usually ask a person to at least read *Victory Over the Darkness* before we meet for our first session. If they struggle with reading, as Jennifer did (which is often a symptom of demonic harassment), then I take them through the Steps to Freedom first and follow up with assignments, such as reading the book or listening to the tapes on the same subject.

Let me emphasize again that I don't assume anything regarding spiritual conflicts. What is needed is a safe means to spiritually check it out. It is no different than going to a medical doctor and having your blood and urine checked. The church needs to assume the responsibility for spiritual diagnosis and resolution.

Seeing deliverance as something you do for a person will usually result in problems. You may effect a person's freedom by casting out a demon, but it is very possible that it will return and the final state will be even worse. When Jennifer did the confessing, renouncing, forgiving, etc., she learned the nature of the battle by going through the process. Instead of bypassing her mind where the real battle was, I appealed to her mind and helped her to assume responsibility for choosing truth.

Jennifer's comments on prescription drugs are appropriate. Using drugs to cure the body is commendable, but using drugs to cure the soul is deplorable. Her ability to think was so impaired that she couldn't process anything. I often see people in this condition and it is extremely frustrating. However, I never go against the advice of a medical doctor. I strongly caution people not to go off prescription drugs too fast, or serious side effects will occur. Jennifer did go off too quickly after her first visit with me and that may have contributed to her subsequent relapse.

Some Don't Want Freedom

Spiritually healthy people will have a hard time understanding that others may not always want to get free from their lifestyle of bondage. I have come across many people who don't want to get rid of their "friends." Once, after walking through the Steps to Freedom with a pastor's wife, I sensed that her freedom wasn't complete. She looked at me and asked, "Now what?" I paused for a moment and said, "Tell it to go." A quizzical look came on her face and she responded, "In the name of the Lord Jesus Christ, I command you to leave my presence." Instantly she was free. The next day she confided that the presence was saying to her mind, "You're not going to just send me away after all the years we have been together, are you?" It was playing on her sympathy.

One young man said a voice was pleading not to make him go because he didn't want to go to hell. The demon wanted to stay so he could go to heaven with him. I asked the young man to pray, asking God to reveal the true nature of the voice. As soon as he had finished praying, he cried out in disgust. I really don't know what he saw or heard, but the evil nature of it was very obvious. These are not harmless spirit guides; they are counterfeit spirits seeking to discredit God and promote allegiance to Satan. They are destroyers who will tear apart a family, church or ministry.

Binging and Purging

Eating disorders are a plight of our age. The sick philosophies of our society have given godlike status to the body. Young girls are often obsessed with appearance as the standard of self-worth. Instead of finding identity in the inner person, they find it in the outer person. Rather than focus on the development of character, they focus on appearance, performance and status. Satan capitalizes on this wrong pursuit of happiness and self-esteem.

Compounding the problem is the rise of sexual abuse and rape. Many girls and young women who are addicted to eating disorders have been sexually victimized. Lacking a gospel, the secular agencies have no way to completely free these people from their past. Knowing who they are in Christ and the absolute necessity of forgiveness is what brings freedom, but they still have to deal with the lies Satan has been using on them.

One young lady was taking seventy-five laxatives a day. Being a graduate of an excellent Christian college, she wasn't dumb. Yet reasoning with her had proved futile. Eating disorder units had stemmed the tide of weight loss by using strong behavioral controls. When I talked with her I asked, "This has nothing to do with eating, does it?" "No," she responded. Then I said, "You're defecating to purge yourself from evil, aren't you?" She nodded in agreement. I asked her to repeat after me, "I renounce defecating in order to purge myself of evil, and I announce that only the blood of Jesus cleanses me from all unrighteousness." She stopped taking laxatives for a short time, but in this case as in Jennifer's, she didn't have the total picture and failed to take advantage of the support she needed.

Another woman said she had purged all her life, just as her mother had. She said she did not consciously plan to do it, and that it was a little joke with her teen daughters that she could vomit into a paper cup while driving and never cross over the line on the road. When I asked her why she was throwing up, she said she felt cleansed afterward. I asked her to repeat after me, "I renounce the lie that throwing up will cleanse me. I believe only in the cleansing work of Christ on the cross." Afterward she immediately cried out, "Oh my God, that's it, isn't it? Only Jesus can cleanse me from my sin." She said that she saw in her mind a vision of the cross.

That is also why people cut themselves. They are trying to purge themselves of evil. It's a spiritual counterfeit, a lie of Satan, that we can be the god of our lives and effect our own cleansing. Remember the 450 prophets of Baal who came up against Elijah? They cut themselves (1 Kings 18:28). Travel around the world and you will witness many pagan religions where they cut themselves during religious ceremonies. It is necessary to reveal that lie and renounce it. In many cases the person isn't aware of why he does it, so asking why may be counterproductive. Jennifer was trying to cut out her heart, believing that it was evil. She also shared that she was cutting herself to get in touch with reality, believing that live people bleed. The young woman taking laxatives immediately started crying after renouncing the lie. After she gained her composure, I asked what she was thinking. She said, "I can't believe all the lies I have believed."

It is important to note that not all of those who cut themselves have eating disorders, and many who have eating disorders don't cut themselves.

I received an insightful letter from a lady who found tremendous release from going through the Steps to Freedom, but the pastor had not addressed her eating disorder at that time. She wrote:

> Dear Neil:
> I just finished reading *The Seduction of Our Children*, which I found very eye opening in many areas. In chapter 13, I was reading through the steps for children when I noticed a separate section for eating disorders. As I was reading, my heart was pierced with a severe pain, yet there was also a sigh of relief. Your words described what my life has been like since grade school.
> Earlier this year I went through the Steps to Freedom with a pastor, and I was a totally different person. Yet, the

one thing that didn't seem right was the struggle I was continuing to have with my physical appearance. That subject hadn't come up during my counseling session.

As I read your description of a typical person with an eating disorder, I just wept before the Lord. It started for me by cutting myself, then I became anorexic, then bulimic, and eventually a mixture of all three.

I read through the renouncing and announcing that you stated and agreed with a friend in prayer about it. God is so good to me. For whatever reason it was overlooked, the enemy meant it for evil to keep me in bondage to an area that had run most of my life. God used your book to add this step of freedom in my life. Thank you so much.

The Need to Be Believed

These people are desperately looking for someone who will believe them, who understand what is going on. They know enough not to share too much of the bizarre thoughts and images with people who don't understand. In Jennifer's case, when she finally did share part of her story, people didn't really believe her and some don't to this day. They see her wholeness as a fluke. Counselors must recognize the reality of Satan's tactics, that we truly do not "fight" against flesh and blood, "but against the rulers, against the powers, against the world forces of this darkness, against the spiritual forces of wickedness in the heavenly places" (Ephesians 6:12).

Aftercare

Jennifer's thoughts on aftercare are choice. The need to have a friend to call and be accountable to can't be stressed enough. We were never intended by God to live alone; we need each other. And Jennifer needed to continue with counseling to help her adjust to a new life. In many ways, she had not developed as others do and needs now to mature into wholeness. Freedom does not constitute maturity. People like Jennifer are developing new habit patterns of thought and it takes time to reprogram their minds.

Her counselors provided her with the support she

needed to survive, and they are good people who would have done anything to help her. Nobody has all the answers. First and foremost, we need the Lord, but we also need each other.

Effective Prayer for Others

I think of the pastors who try to help people like Jennifer. Most pastors haven't had formal training in counseling, and few have had seminary training that equipped them to deal with the kingdom of darkness. Desperate people come with overwhelming needs, knowing that their only hope is the Lord. Sometimes the only pastoral weapon at their disposal is prayer, so they pray. But often they see very little happen in response to their prayer of faith. That can be very discouraging.

Most Christians are aware of the passage in James that instructs those who are sick to call the elders who are to pray and anoint with oil. I believe the church should be doing this, but I think we have overlooked some very important concepts and the order implied in James: "Is anyone among you suffering? Let him pray" (5:13). The primary person who needs to pray is the sufferer. Hurting people who saw me when I was pastoring asked for prayer. Of course, I prayed for them, but the one who really needed to pray was the person who was seeing me.

After walking a social worker through the Steps to Freedom, the change in her countenance was so noticeable that I encouraged her to visit the rest room and take a good look in the mirror. She was glowing when she returned to my office. As she reflected on the resolution of her spiritual conflicts, she said, "I always thought somebody else had to pray for me." That is a very common misconception. In the Steps to Freedom, the counselee is the one doing most of the praying.

We can't have a secondary relationship with God. We may need a third party to facilitate the reconciliation of two personalities, but they won't be reconciled by what the facilitator does. They will only be reconciled by the concessions made by the principal parties. In spiritual resolution, God doesn't make concessions in order for us to be reconciled to Him. The Steps to Freedom lay out the "concessions" that we have to make in order to assume our responsibility.

"Is anyone among you sick? Let him call for the elders of the church" (5:14). Again the responsibility to take the initiative is upon the one who is sick. The primary responsibility to get well is always placed on the sick person. I doubt that we will ever be effective in trying to heal a hurting humanity that doesn't want to get well. The Steps to Freedom only work if the person wants to be well and will assume his own responsibility.

Mark records the incident when Jesus sent His disciples on ahead of Him in a boat. The wind came up, and the disciples ended up in the middle of the sea, "straining at the oars." As Jesus walked on the sea, "He intended to pass by them" (Mark 6:48). I believe that Jesus intends to pass by the self-sufficient. If we want to do it ourselves, He will let us. When the disciples called upon Jesus, He came to them. When the sick call the elders, they should also come.

James continues, "Therefore, confess your sins to one another, and pray for one another, so that you may be healed. The effective prayer of a righteous man can accomplish much" (5:16). I believe the prayers of our pastors will be effective when the people are willing to confess their sins. The Steps to Freedom are a fierce moral inventory. I have heard people confess incredible atrocities as they go through the steps. My role is to give them the assurance that God answers prayer and forgives His repentant children.

I am most confident in prayer after I have taken a person through the Steps to Freedom. John writes, "The one who practices sin is of the devil; for the devil has sinned from the beginning. The Son of God appeared for this purpose, that He might destroy the works of the devil" (1 John 3:8). I believe we are perfectly in God's will when we ask Him to restore a life damaged by Satan. That damage could be physical, emotional or spiritual.

The order is "seek first the Kingdom of God," then all the other things will be added unto us. A young lady approached me in a conference with a cheerful "Hi!" "Hi," I responded. She said, "You don't recognize me, do you?" I didn't, and even after she reminded me that I had counseled with her a year earlier, I still didn't recognize her. She had changed that much. Like Jennifer, her appearance and countenance were totally different, a beautiful demonstration of change in a person "seeking first the kingdom of God." What a difference freedom in Christ makes!

5

Nancy:
Female Sexual Abuse and Freedom

The sin, confess, sin, confess, sin, "I give up" cycle is most common in sexual bondages. Suppose the neighbor's dog got into your yard because you left the gate open. The dog's jaw is now clamped around the calf of your leg. Would you beat on yourself or the dog?

Painfully aware that we left the door open to sin, we cry out to God for forgiveness. Guess what God does? He forgives us! He said He would—but the dog is still there. Rather than the sin, confess routine, the complete biblical perspective is: sin, confess, *resist*: "Submit therefore to God. Resist the devil and he will flee from you" (James 4:7).

In our western world, we operate as though the only players in the drama are ourselves and God. That isn't true. If it's only you and God, then either you or God are going to have to take the rap for an awful lot of havoc in this world. I believe that God is not the author of confusion and death, but of order and life. The god of this world is the chief architect of rebellion, sin, sickness and death. He is the father of lies (John 8:44).

However, "the devil made me do it" is not a part of my theology or practice. It is our responsibility not to let sin reign in our mortal body (Romans 6:12). But treating those in bondage as the principal culprits, and throwing them out because they can't get their act together, is the height of pharisaic judgment and human rejection.

If you witness a little girl being sexually molested because she left the door open and evil intruders took advantage of her carelessness, would you overlook the abusers and confront only the girl? If you did, the little girl will conclude that there is something evil about herself. That's what Nancy and many others like her have experienced. Let's learn from her story.

*   *   *

Nancy's Story

We looked like a normal, happy family.

Both of my parents were young and non-Christians. They had been married two years, and their marriage was rocky, when I was born. Later two brothers and a sister were added, and photos from that time showed that we looked like a normal, happy family. My dad was handsome and my mother was nice looking, too. Mostly the pictures are of the family all dressed up for church on Easter Sunday—we never went any other time.

We moved a lot, and I attended eight different schools before attending high school—two different high schools.

My father would tell me that I was his special girl. Then he would touch me.

My father had a drug and alcohol problem and was in and out of jail for stealing to buy the things he needed in order to feed his addiction. He even broke open my piggy bank for whatever money I had and once sold all of the lamps in the house. He would leave for a couple of days at a time and then come home smashed and abusive, breaking furniture, pictures and glassware. This was not an uncommon thing; whenever my father got mad, things were destroyed.

My father told me when I was three that I could sleep in his room while my mother was at work. I remember lying in my parents' bed and my dad talking to me like I was his wife. He told me that he loved me more than he did my mother and that I was his special girl. Then he would touch me sexually. I really had no idea what was going on, only that this made Daddy happy and then he would be nice to me. He told me that I should never tell my mother about this because she wouldn't understand. It was then that I started masturbating, usually several times a day.

This was a confusing time for me. Sometimes I was torn between my parents, but on other nights, when my mother was home, my father would beat me and throw me against the wall. One night he took a blanket and threw it over my entire body and then sat on the blanket. I couldn't breathe or see any light. At first my mother just laughed, but then she yelled at my dad and told him to get up. That experience was one of the first times I remember being outside of myself and watching what was going on.

Another time, my dad got my baby brother and me drunk. He would give us tastes of whatever he was drinking and then spin us around and watch us walk funny.

About every two or three months my mom would leave my dad and we would spend some time at my grand-parents' home until my dad would say, "I'm sorry; I won't ever do it again." So we would move back with him. During those times of separation I would always be with my mom, and I was glad. I was so afraid of being totally alone with my father.

The house was totaled, worse than usual. My dad was standing over us with a gun.

One time when I was about five, Dad came home and there was the usual broken furniture and pictures, but this time was different. It was late at night and mom and I were up, but we were not packing to leave as we often did. On this particular night we were crouched in a corner of their bedroom. The house was totaled, worse than usual, and my dad was standing over us with a gun pointed at my mother's head. He said, "This is it. I'm going to pull the trigger." My mom hugged me tightly and pleaded with him not to kill her. I was crying, and I heard the trigger snap, but no explosion. Mom had thrown away the bullets and the gun that my dad thought was loaded was empty, although Mom wasn't sure whether he had gotten more bullets or not.

At that, my dad became even more angry and picked up my mom and threw her across the room. Mom told me to run next door, so I did. The police came and took my dad away, and I stayed at the neighbors' house, sleeping in a strange bed all alone and crying like I had never cried before. I wanted my mom to hold me, but she wasn't there. I don't know where she went, but whenever things got really bad I always had to stay somewhere else without my mom. I still don't understand where she went and why she didn't want me with her.

I loved my mom, but I never felt she loved me. I knew my dad loved me, but he scared me.

Another time, my dad had a knife and my mother had a broken bottle and they were fighting. I remember battling in my mind about which one I wanted to win. I loved my mom, but I never felt that she loved me. I knew my dad loved me, but he scared me. That time, Dad did cut Mom's throat and beat her up, and a neighbor had to take her to the hospital where she stayed for several days. I was, of course, at a friend's house . . . again alone.

I thought my parents loved animals more than people. One time my dad brought home a dog that had been mistreated. My parents felt so bad for this dog—they loved him, fed him extra and talked about how awful his past owners had been. I remember being jealous of the dog, wishing that my parents would be good "owners" of me.

By the time I was six, my dad had been in and out of jail several times and my mother finally left him. We moved in with my grandparents for a couple of years and then, later, into another house in the same town.

I talked to myself constantly, saying how much I needed to masturbate in order to feel better. I would dream of boys in class at school and pretend we were making love. One time I was masturbating while watching TV, and my mother came into the room and watched. I didn't see her at first, but when I did, she just smiled at me and told me this was normal.

There were times in the bathtub when I would travel outside of myself and dream I was drowning myself. It felt both good and scary all at the same time. I'd fill up the tub as high as I could, get in and see myself under the water, face up and dead.

Shadows would come out of grandma's closet. I would hear voices and things would move around the room.

I spent as much time as I could at my grandmother's house and saw strange things: shadows coming out of grandma's closet, voices and noises, and things moving around the room. Once my toy broom flew across my bedroom. These things startled me at first, but after awhile I enjoyed trying to make things move myself.

My grandmother gave me a Ouija board, and my brother and I played with it. It was about this time that I asked my brother to sleep with me, and we kissed and held hands. I loved him so much and felt there was no other way to really show him that I cared. (Oh, how I hate you, Satan!)

I was given a dog and would look at him and think, "I love you truly." I would let him lick me and for awhile it would feel good, but then I would get depressed. One day, I looked at him and wondered what it would be like for him to be dead. Only a few minutes later, he ran out in the road and was hit by a car and killed instantly. I remember having other dreams come true as well.

When I was about seven, I attended a neighborhood church. I enjoyed the songs and the people seemed so nice, but I can't remember anyone ever asking who I was or why I was there by myself.

She wrote stories about friendly ghosts.
So I thought the ghosts I was seeing
in her house were good also.

My grandmother and grandfather didn't sleep together. I learned later that my grandfather had an affair and my grandmother said that he could stay, but they never slept together again, so I would sleep with my grandmother. She wrote stories and would tell them to me, usually stories about friendly ghosts, so I thought the ghosts I was seeing in her house were good.

My grandfather loved me and told me I was his favorite grandchild. I slept with him, too, but he never touched me inappropriately or yelled at me or hurt me in any way. We would talk together at the dinner table and play games together, and he would play his guitar and sing for me. Even though there were strange things at their house, this was the closest thing to a happy family in my experience.

My mother remarried and we moved away. The first few years of their marriage seemed normal. We got spankings, but not beatings. I was in Brownies, tap dancing, gymnastics, and I did well at school. I still heard voices saying, "You're ugly and stupid. This is going to end and your real father is going to come and get you."

I started having dreams about dying and would lie in bed crying out to God for help, "Please let there be something other than death, something beyond death." I dreamed that my grandparents were going to die, that I would never see them again. I dreamed my mother would die. It became such an obsession that I couldn't get to sleep unless I thought of someone in my family dying, and then I would cry myself to sleep.

I went to a church with a Christian friend and went forward during the altar call, wanting so much for someone to love me and help me, but this was not the time or the place. The counselor said that I needed to be "slain under the cross" so that I could speak in another language. My friend said that I would fall over afterwards and that I shouldn't be afraid.

There were about thirty people around me who all started to pray, some in tongues and some not. It was hot and I just wanted to go home, so I thought I would talk some gibberish and fall over, which I did. Everyone was so excited that I was now a "Christian." I knew I had fooled them and was confused, wondering if Christians were fakes.

We would play in the greenhouse, and we would hold hands and kiss.

While in grade school, I had a babysitter only a few years older than me who would take off her clothes and my clothes and we would lay on each other on the living room floor. Sometimes I spent the night at her house and she would play with me, naked.

In the summers I visited my grandparents' home and the summer after I finished fifth grade, I took a friend with me. I had never had homosexual desires before, but that summer it was different. We played in the greenhouse and I told her she was my wife, or I her's, and we would hold hands and kiss. One thing led to another and we would end up on the floor rolling around together until I would end up masturbating. I don't think she ever did and she seemed scared, but she was always willing to play the game several times a day.

When we returned home, we went into the bushes and tried the game again, but this time it didn't seem right and we never did it again. We stayed friends throughout our school years but never again mentioned our summer together.

The next year I took another friend to grandmother's house. This time we stayed in the bedroom and read magazines and acted out the stories in them.

The voice would say, "You fool.
You are so stupid and ugly,
no one will want you."

By the time I was in junior high, my mom and stepdad were fighting more and more. I felt guilty about their fights, but mostly about my masturbation problem. I couldn't tell anyone or ask if this was normal, though I already knew it couldn't be. I tried my hardest to stop, but there was always that voice saying, "No, it's all right. Everyone does it." Then, afterwards, the same voice would say, "You fool. You are so stupid and ugly, no one will want you."

When I was in high school, lying became a big part of my life. I wanted to have friends and fun, but I saw myself as stupid and inferior, so I would make up stories to make myself look and feel better.

I dated a lot and would let the boys do whatever they wanted with me, up to the point of actually having intercourse—I could finish that feeling at home. Of course, the guys didn't know that, so I became known as a big tease. Several told me that I drove them crazy for sex and that made me feel so down on myself: guilty, dirty inside and out, ugly, and again a failure.

Finally the inevitable happened. I did have intercourse with a boy in the front seat of his car outside a drive-in. It wasn't really painful; it wasn't anything. We drove back to his house because his dad was an alcoholic and never at home. We took a shower together and I did sex dances for him.

When I got home, my stepdad was waiting up for me as he always did. We didn't talk much, just looked at each other, and I went to bed, feeling numb as I fell asleep thinking about all that had happened that night. The next morning I called the boy and told him I never wanted to see him again, and I told everyone at school what a loser he was.

Later I asked my mom if you could wear white to your wedding if you were not a virgin. She just said, "You can wear whatever you want." I felt so rejected—I wish she would have asked me what had happened.

I remembered how good it felt as a child
in church and felt that way again.

After one of our family moves I rode the bus to my new high school. I had decided I would not make friends with anyone because I hated it there and I hated my stepdad for making us move again. A blond, bubbly cheerleader got on the bus and sat next to me, holding a trophy and smiling from ear to ear. I just glared at her. I was into cheerleading and pep week at the school I just moved from, and I didn't need her to remind me of what I had left behind.

She talked all the way to school and ended up inviting me to her church youth group. I had no idea what a church youth group was and I certainly wasn't going to make friends with her. However, we rode the bus together for several weeks and finally I agreed to go.

I was surprised to find a group of kids singing, laughing and reading Bibles. I remembered how good it felt in church when I was a child and felt that way again. My voices told me, "No! These kids won't like you. You are stupid for being here." But the girl I met on the bus continued to be my friend, and by the end of that school year I asked Christ to come into my life and was baptized.

I was so on fire for the Lord. I had finally found someone who would never leave me, hit me or make me do bad things—someone who would always love me. I told everyone about Jesus and walked around the house with my Bible, quoting verses. I began a Bible study with my brothers and we would pray together and talk about Christ's love.

I took all the money I could find
in the house and ran away.

Then when I was in my senior year of high school, my mom and stepdad had a very violent fight. I was frozen with fear and felt that I couldn't stand to see what had happened with my birth father re-enacted, so I took all the money I could find in the house and ran away. I drove to another state and moved in with a boy I had met earlier. The voices within me started up again, saying, "You slut! You call yourself a Christian?"

After awhile, my boyfriend and I broke up and I went back home, but my stepdad didn't want me to stay. One night I attended a ball game at a local Bible college. Through all that had been happening, I wore a facade and told people that I was a Christian and that God is great.

However, during the game, I was thinking about my situation: how I had been living with a guy, had come back from running away and now had no place to live. Just then, a girl next to me asked if I needed a place to live. I asked if she could read my mind and told her that I did. I moved in with her and two other girls and found out that she was a lesbian and thought I was cute. But that was one relationship I never did pursue.

Some of the things in my life were hard for him to take, but he told me that he loved me anyway.

One of the girls I lived with had a brother I liked, but she was trying to guard his innocence and really didn't want me to date him. However, we started to go out together, and it was a different relationship than I had ever had before. I knew Jim cared about me—really cared!

Shortly after we were engaged, I cheated on him. I felt so guilty that I gave back the engagement ring, but he wouldn't break off the relationship. I was all mixed up, still masturbating and not eating well. In my heart I wanted him to love me and stay with me, but I was mean to him.

I decided that the man I would marry would have to know the truth about me, so I shared my past with him. He had come from a very strict, sheltered Christian home, and some of the things in my life were hard for him to take, but he told me that he loved me anyway. Seven months later we were married.

We never slept together before we were married, but afterwards we had a very abnormal sexual relationship. I was addicted to sex, not only with my husband but also with masturbation. This created tension, so we fought and I began to feel dirty and alone again.

Our first ten years of marriage were turbulent. Jim attended Bible college, worked for a major company for seven years, and then officially went into ministry. I was excited to be a minister's wife and put high expectations on myself to be perfect and always available to help others.

We had two children, but I wasn't much of a mom. I hit them a lot and was depressed easily. I felt like my life was a waste; suicide was a daily thought. I would alternate between fits of rage and asking forgiveness. I wanted to be close to God but never felt that I was.

When I became pregnant a third time a big part of me wanted to have an abortion, but a small part of me said, "Love this child." My husband was excited about that pregnancy, but we fought even more and my mood swings went out of control. The baby came and I didn't know how I could possibly take care of another child. All I wanted was to be out of this life. I was depressed and bored, and felt ugly and stupid, unwanted and lonely.

Meanwhile, at church and in the meetings everyone seemed to like me. I was usually the life of the party, but that was a cover. No one really knew me.

I came very close to having an affair with one of the deacons who was married to my best friend. We never got beyond the talk stage, but I was very tempted and so confused. A voice inside of me said, "Go for it. No one will ever know." But another part of me said, "Be faithful to your husband." After that I became disinterested in sex with Jim, but still had the problem with masturbation.

I could see shadows darting across the hall. I tried to kill myself.

My stepfather died and we brought his favorite chair home. When I sat in the chair and looked down our hallway, I could see shadows darting from the kids' rooms to the bedroom across the hall. At first I thought I was just tired, but then I learned my husband and others saw them too.

One night a figure stood at the end of my bed and stared at me. It was tall and dark with a short-looking child standing beside it. These apparitions occurred off and on for several months. I got more and more depressed and tried to kill myself several times with pills. I talked about death and sang songs about dying. I told my husband that was the only way I would ever have peace—then things would be quiet and I would be with God.

As I became increasingly morose, Jim began staying away at night and would take the kids away for the weekend. He didn't know what to do, so he ran and hid from it all. I would stay in bed for two or three days at a time with the door locked and a sign on the door telling everyone to go away. Meanwhile, Jim would make excuses for me at church, telling everyone I was sick.

Several times our oldest child called for an ambulance thinking that I was dying. They would take me to the emergency room, run some tests, tell me I was fine and send me home again.

Once a minister's name came to mind and I cried out in desperation for someone to get him to help me. Jim wasn't home, but our babysitter was there and she called him. He prayed with me and referred me to a Christian counselor whom I saw for three months.

The counselor began by saying I was a Christian and he was a Christian, but that this was not a spiritual problem. He said I had been abused by several men in my life, I was too busy, and I wasn't facing the child inside me. A small voice inside of me said, "But where is Christ in all of this?" I knew the answers must be in Him, but I just couldn't get there. I finally stopped going to the counselor.

One of our children began seeing "things" and having terrible dreams.

One day I decided it was time for action, so I took my father's chair to a flea market and sold it. After that, we all stopped seeing ghosts in our home. I quit my job because I had been seeing ghosts there, too. At this point I started having a daily Bible study.

Jim and I started to get along better and things became nearer normal, though I still really wanted to die so he could find a better wife and our kids could have a good mom who didn't cringe when they said "I love you, Mom." Then Jim was offered another job and we moved, desperately hoping this fresh start would help us.

In our new location, one of our children began seeing "things" and having terrible dreams. He wouldn't be left alone. He would see a blond man run through his room and out the door. One night when he was four, he said, "I need the Lord to live in me." He asked Christ into his life and not only did the apparitions and dreams go away, he was also instantly healed of serious asthma attacks and went off all of his medicines and a breathing machine! If you ask him about that today, he will say, "God healed me."

After that brief time of near normalcy, the new job turned into a disaster. I started masturbating again, fighting and lying. My husband was fired and we moved to another location where God wonderfully provided a home and another job on the staff of a church. With the excitement of the new situation we were fine for awhile, but then depression set in again. I couldn't function and again I just wanted to die. I had no friends; there was no one I could talk to. Who would understand voices, ghosts, deep depression and an obsession with dying? I lived a double life—trying to help at church, even introducing some to the Lord, while at home I was a hysterical, raging person. I was fooling everyone but my family. I felt like I was going crazy.

A doctor diagnosed my problem as PMS and said there was a new pill that would help. I believed that a Christian could have physical problems, but in my case the problem was in my mind and I knew that somehow I needed to end this mental torment.

I was afraid . . . afraid to take a shower for fear that the shower curtain would wrap itself around me and kill me . . . afraid to answer the phone, not wanting to talk with anyone . . . afraid to take responsibility, no longer being the person who loved to plan and organize and conduct big events . . . afraid of the faces in the mirror in my bedroom . . . and afraid to drive at night because figures and snakes would appear in the headlights.

Prayers were being answered and our ministry at the church was growing.

At a Bible bookstore, I found a prayer notebook and Jim bought if for me. He was so desperate for me to get better that he would do anything. All through this time, he was telling me that God would bring us through this, was praying for me constantly and, this time, not running away into his work.

I brought the prayer binder home and began to have daily morning Bible studies. I had preached having daily Bible study to others, but had never been able to keep it up myself. I began a regular time with God and it was wonderful. The negative voices stopped, for awhile I stopped masturbating, prayers were being answered and our ministry at the church was growing.

I felt so scared and sick that I wished Neil would cancel.

In preparation for a "Resolving Personal and Spiritual Conflicts Conference" at our church, a film was shown where Neil spoke and some people gave testimonies. As I watched, I started getting sick and wanted to run out, but I stayed because of what people would think. On the way home that night I told Jim that I didn't want to go to the conference and that I was better now. I felt that as long as I studied and prayed every morning I would be fine. We talked about it and then dropped the subject. Since the conference was still two months away, I felt safe.

In the weeks before the conference there was a lot of excitement at church. Everyone was talking about how great it sounded and they were inviting friends. I decided that I would go just to learn how to help others and to support Jim. Then the turmoil started again—I couldn't pray, I became angry easily and I started masturbating again. I felt so scared and sick that I wished Neil would cancel.

The first night of the conference I sat there acting cool, taking notes and pretending it didn't affect me. But by the third night I couldn't concentrate and nothing made sense. I felt that I would either throw up or dissolve in tears. I heard voices, had terrible thoughts and was going downhill fast, especially when Neil talked about rape.

Jim made an appointment for me with Neil, and when he told me about it I started shaking. When the morning of the appointment came, I told Jim there was no way I was going to see some conceited speaker who would just say that I am lying and needed to snap out of it.

Jim prayed a lot and convinced me to go with him to the conference and then to the appointment. That morning I cried through the sessions. Finally I could take it no longer and went out to sit in the car. This was by far the worst internal struggle of my entire life. I found myself saying, "Why did he come? Doesn't he know that I don't need his help? I like being this way. I'm just fine. Why can't he go away? He will ruin everything." I especially kept hearing that last thought, *He will ruin everything.*

Then another part of me said, "What could he ruin?" I felt such fear that I thought of driving my car right through the fence in front of me and escaping, but I didn't. I had no place to hide. I wanted help so badly but doubted that Neil would have any answers. Then I got mad. I hated Neil; he was the enemy. I would go to this stupid appointment, but I would win.

---

*I told Neil that I didn't like him,
and that this wasn't going to work.*

Jim found me in the car and we went to lunch with a friend. Then we went back to the conference and before I knew it, I was sitting in a room with Neil and a couple from his staff. What happened during the next two hours I will never forget, and I will never be the same.

First I told Neil that I didn't like him and that this wasn't going to work. I told him some of the things about my family in a very matter-of-fact way. Then I went through the first prayer in the Steps to Freedom with no problem, even though I didn't know what I read. But when it came time to renounce all my cultic, occultic and non-Christian experiences, I couldn't pray. I felt like throwing up, my vision went in and out, and I felt like I was choking and couldn't breathe. I remember Neil quietly telling Satan to release me, affirming that I was a child of God. I felt calmed and continued to go through the prayers.

When we came to the forgiveness part, I told Neil I had no one to forgive, that I loved everyone except him right now. He told me to pray and ask God to bring to mind people I needed to forgive. Names came to mind I hadn't thought about in years. When I started praying to forgive them, I cried and cried, and this time the tears felt good. I felt like a heavy block was being lifted from my chest and head.

We went through the other prayers and I felt progressively better. I could breathe and I felt loved. When we had finished, Neil suggested that I go into the rest room and take a good look at myself in the mirror. I did, and for the first time in my life, I liked what I saw! I said, "I like you, Nancy. In fact, I love you." I looked into my eyes and was happy. I felt that because of Jesus, there was a truly good person there. That was the first time I have ever looked in the mirror without feeling disgust for myself.

That night I had to drive a three-hour distance to a brother's graduation. Jim couldn't join me because of his responsibilities at the conference.

I looked at the sky and said,
"Praise God, I really am free!"

I had not driven much in the dark because of the images I would see, usually white snakes jumping up at the car. One time I saw a burning car engulfed in flames, but when I got to the spot there was nothing. I have seen people hitchhiking and then suddenly there was no one there. So driving at night brought great fear. But that night, during the entire three-hour drive, I saw nothing. Praise God!

The next day, along with 28,000 others, I attended the graduation ceremony. Before this, crowds would cause me to panic. I would feel like I was trapped and couldn't get out, like I was choking, like I couldn't breathe, and it was as though the sky was falling around me. That day, however, I felt none of those symptoms. In fact, it wasn't until I was walking out of the stadium with people all around me that I realized the fear was gone. I looked at the sky and said, "Praise God, I really am free!"

When I was praying with Neil, what I appreciated most is that it wasn't a typical counseling appointment—it was a time with God. Neil guided me through the prayers and kept me going, but it was God who delivered me from Satan's clutches; it was God who cleaned the house of my mind.

I looked around our bedroom. It was quiet, really quiet. No voices.

The first morning in our home after the conference, I looked around our bedroom and listened. It was quiet, really quiet . . . no voices, and they haven't come back! Occasionally I have felt frustrated, but now I know how to deal with it.

Since then, our youngest child had some fears and bad dreams. Instead of praying in fear, we talked about who he is in Christ. Our son said, "Hey! Satan's afraid of me. He had just better watch out 'cuz I'm a child of God."

My husband and I took a couple through the Steps to Freedom. They, too, are now free.

A few months later some missionary friends stayed with us for a week. The wife had been harassed in various ways including depression and thoughts of suicide. Jim and I took them through the Steps to Freedom and they, too, are free!

Since I found my freedom in Christ, I can say "I love you" to my husband and not hear thoughts of *No you don't*, or *This marriage will never last.* For a long time now, I have not had depression. I haven't yelled uncontrollably at my children. I'm not afraid of the shower curtain. And masturbation is no longer a problem. Jim and I have been able to lead many of our friends at church through the Steps to Freedom, and we are enjoying seeing freedom spread. Praise God, I really am free!

*   *   *

Do They Hate You?

You may be wondering why Nancy, Sandy and others expressed hatred toward me. I'm happy to share that's not their true feeling because that's not really them. Satan isn't pleased with what I'm saying and the fact that I am helping people take back ground where he has had a stronghold. If this happens when you're helping someone, just ignore those comments and continue. After they complete the steps and are free, they often express a great love toward you. Remember Anne's comment in chapter 2? She said, "I immediately had a great love-jump in my heart toward you, Neil."

Demonic Transference

If demonic influence can be passed from one person to another, it will take place during illicit sex more than any other time that I am aware of. Every sexually abused person that I have worked with has had major spiritual difficulties. Compulsive masturbation from the age of three is not "normal" sexual development, especially for girls. But it is a common stronghold for those who have been sexually violated. These women are often in deep condemnation, both from the enemy and themselves, and gladly turn from masturbation when they understand how to renounce its entrance point and stand against Satan.

The stronghold is greater if the sexual abuser is a parent. Parents are the authority in the home. They are supposed to provide the spiritual protection that every child needs in order to develop spiritually, socially, mentally and physically. Parents who are in bondage will pass on their iniquity to the next generation. When they become the abuser, they directly open the gate for spiritual assault in their child. Instead of being the spiritual umbrella of protection they are opening the floodgates of devastation.

Guarding What God Entrusts to You

The underlying principle is stewardship. We are to be good stewards of whatever God entrusts to us (1 Corinthians 4:1-3). In *The Seduction of Our Children,* I develop this concept much further. Every parent should know what it means to dedicate their children to the Lord and how to pray for their spiritual protection. As parents we have no greater stewardship than the lives of the little children God has entrusted to us.

Sexual Union/Spiritual Bond

Every church has a story of a lovely young lady who gets involved with the wrong man. After having sex with him, she can't seem to break away. Everybody tries to convince her that he isn't any good for her. Sometimes even her close friends side with her parents and she really knows the relationship is sick since he treats her like mud. Why doesn't she just tell him to take a hike? Because the sexual union has created a "spiritual" bond. Unless she breaks that, she will always feel bound to him by something she doesn't even understand.

A pastor called me one day and said, "If you can't help this young girl I've been counseling, she will be hospitalized in a psych ward." For two years she had a sick relationship with a boy who was dealing drugs and generally treating her as a sex object. The mental assault she was experiencing was so vivid that she couldn't understand why others couldn't hear the voices she was hearing. After hearing her story, I asked her what she would do if I required her to leave this guy and never have anything to do with him again. She started to shake and said, "I would probably have to leave this session."

I took her through the Steps to Freedom, encouraging her to: ask forgiveness for using her body as an instrument of unrighteousness, renounce all sexual experiences that God revealed to her, and acknowledge that her body is the temple of the Holy Spirit. Her newfound freedom was immediately evident to me and my prayer partners in the room. Without any coaching she said she was also free from the boy, and to my knowledge she never saw him again.

God Wants His Children Free

I have found it necessary for all sexual sins to be renounced. I usually have such people pray, asking the Lord to reveal to their minds all the sexual sins and partners with whom they have been involved, whether they were the victim or the perpetrator. It is amazing how experiences will come flooding back to their minds. God wants His children free. When they renounce the experience, they are specifically renouncing Satan and all his works and all his ways, and breaking those ties. When they ask forgiveness, they are choosing to walk in the light with God. The power of Satan and sin has then been broken and fellowship with the Lord is beautifully restored.

6

Doug:
Male Sexual Abuse
and Freedom

Feelings of disgust rise rapidly to the average mind when images of sexual perversion are entertained. Suppose that was your own self-perception, and you were in full-time ministry. To add insult to injury, add the self-concept of being a bastard raised in a racially mixed home with all the social rejection that unfortunately follows.

How would you feel toward yourself? Would you readily accept the fact that you are a saint who sins, or would you see yourself as a wretched sinner? Would you walk in the light, have fellowship with other believers, and speak the truth in love? Or would you live a lonely life, frightened to death that someone may somehow find out what is really going on inside? Such is the case of our next story.

* * *

Doug's Story

Dad never called me "son."

My mother wasn't married when I was born, but when I was two years old she married a black man. He was a decent person, but he never called me "son," and never said he loved me. Whenever I would go somewhere with both of my parents, it was obvious I was not a product of their marriage, and sometimes I was called "Sambo's little kid."

While I was pre-school age, a woman babysitter took me to her apartment and played sexual games with me. In the ensuing years I did sexual experimentation with other children, was sexually exploited by older girls and boys, and eventually was raped by young men.

I understood my identity to be a "bastard": unplanned, unwanted, an accident. Early on I perceived that my craving for love and acceptance might possibly be met through sex, and that by giving fulfillment to others through sex I could show that my love was not selfish. Thus sex became an obsession and eventually led to perversion.

I tried very hard to gain praise and approval in the "straight" world also, and won many awards and honors at school. But my self-image was at zero, and no one or nothing seemed to help. At age sixteen I became suicidal.

Then one summer I went to camp and met people who genuinely seemed to care. It was there I learned of Jesus' love for me. The promise of that love, combined with a disgust for myself, drew me to receive Him as my Savior. I then knew that my lifestyle was wrong and that I should turn from it, but I had been programmed to it for years and I seemed powerless to change.

Nevertheless, I purposed to follow Christ, praying that somehow, by some miracle, I would become the person I longed to be. I trained for the ministry, graduated from school and threw myself into my work. I think part of my motivation for going into ministry was to give myself to others so they could love me back.

Our marriage relationship was doomed from the start.

After a few years I married a wonderful woman. Our relationship was doomed from the start because invading thoughts of male images and my own past perversion destroyed any possibility of a healthy sexual life. I continually struggled against going back to previous forms of wrongful sex. I turned to masturbation, which I considered "safe" sex because I could control my environment.

My wife was always loyal to me, yet she sensed something was definitely wrong. It wasn't until we were married for ten years that I finally told her a little about my problem. That news was very painful for her, but at the same time she felt relief at finally knowing the truth.

I heard speaker after speaker talk about victory in Jesus and I thought, *That's fine for someone who doesn't have my background. That will work for others, but not for me. I will just have to live with my sin. I'll have heaven later, but for now I'll have to deal with the realities of my past.* I felt locked into a horrible identity; it was a heavy bondage.

> ### If I committed suicide, I hoped it would look like an accident.

I developed a contingency plan in the event that anyone ever found out I had been gay or bisexual. I would drive my car into an oncoming semi-truck. I prepared for that through the years by telling people how I would get very sleepy at the wheel and have to eat snacks to stay awake. If I ever committed suicide, I hoped it would look like an accident and there would be insurance money for my family.

One night in a therapy group, I was hypnotized and told some of my problem—more than I should have. I left with the group's encouragement, but did not feel good about what I had shared with them. I looked for semis on the lonely road home, determined to end my life, but there were none. As I drove into the driveway my children came running to me, and their acceptance and love was so wonderful that I clicked back into reality.

> ### I took a step of moving away from my prison of self-pity.

After some defeats in ministry, I asked counsel from

some older Christian brothers. One of them said, "I hear you saying you are trying very hard to prove you are worthy." That was hard truth, and I immediately went into my pattern of "pity-partying," saying, "Lord, there has never been a person so rejected as me." Then it was as though God spoke aloud to my mind and said, "The only one I ever turned my back on was My own Son who bore your sins on the cross." That was a step toward recovery, of moving away from my prison of self-pity.

Little by little there was growth. God was helping me to see things from a different perspective and I wasn't so controlled by my passions. But the reality that our marriage relationship wasn't all that it should be continued to haunt me.

On a scale of ten, temptations in my
thought life went down to a two.

I had an opportunity to sit under Neil's teaching and heard him speak on spiritual conflict. There I learned some new dimensions of resisting Satan and, on a scale of ten, temptations in my thought life went down to a two. My prayer life became more vibrant and intense. My need for sexual self-gratification diminished until that addiction of a quarter-of-a-century stopped altogether.

Finally I found that I could have a normal relationship with my wife without a videotape playing in my mind of others imposing themselves upon me sexually. It was a wholesome, beautiful thing. All of those changes were taking place without my pursuing them. I happened to sit under Neil's teaching, and the Lord did the rest.

I thought that the only way to destroy
the sin was to destroy the sinner.

Then some difficulties arose, and I realized that I was under attack and needed to go back and reinforce what I had learned. The truth that had helped me in such a variety of ways was the truth of who I am in Christ, defined by my Savior and not by my sin. In Romans, I saw the difference between who I am and my activity: "If I am doing the very thing I do not wish, I am no longer the one doing it, but sin which dwells in me" (Romans 7:20). I was finally able to separate the real me from my actions. The reason I was suicidal all those years was because I had thought the only way to destroy the sin was to destroy the sinner. There was still an ongoing battle between the authority of my experiences versus the authority of Scripture, but I began to be able to live out my true identity by choosing truth and standing against Satan's lies.

I was able to use the help given to me by Neil when I spoke at a weekend church conference. After the last session, there was a testimony time where people began confessing their faults to one another, like a mini-revival. I had never seen anything like it before; it was beautiful to experience.

But even as I spoke at that conference on spiritual conflict, my wife, who was hundreds of miles away, was startled with demonic manifestations in our home. She had to call in friends to support her and pray for her. And that became a pattern for a period of time.

On the plus side: People were being set free through our ministry from bondages that had enslaved them for years. Victims of abuse who had been dysfunctional in their relationships were having their marriages restored; pastors were being freed from problems paralyzing their ministries. At the same time, we found ourselves harassed by Satan and being run ragged by a busy schedule.

During that oppression there was a tidal wave of perverse thoughts.

As I reflect back to the time when I had planned on taking my life but had come home and met my children in the driveway, I realize that many of my memories from the past had been graciously blocked out. But during the demonic oppression that came later, there were flashbacks to perverted behavior and tidal wave after tidal wave of perverse thoughts. Then there would be an onslaught of self-destructive thoughts—that suicide was again the easiest way to get out of all the pressure we were experiencing.

I went in and out of reality, not being able to control it. I became afraid of losing my mind. In the middle of the night, I would awake in a sweat, having dreamed of incredible horror, of killing loved ones and placing their bodies in transparent body bags.

I shared this attack with my brothers in Christ, and a massive amount of prayer went up. I was so weak and vulnerable and I needed the prayer support of God's people to lift that onslaught of demonic depression. Finally it did lift, and I was again able to think objectively and spiritually about the issues.

The strength that I have today is because I don't stand alone.

From experience, I am convinced that no one is ever so strong that he can stand alone. I have a wife who prays for me, a support group of men with whom I meet once a week, a Bible study group at church, and concerned friends and loved ones. We all need a body of believers for encouragement, people who will stand with us against the attacks of the enemy.

I'm looking forward to the challenges ahead. Our ministry continues. My wife and I are still working on some issues in our marriage which haven't been totally resolved, but there is nothing there that God cannot heal. My acceptance in Him is my greatest strength. Because of His unconditional love, I don't have to prove myself worthy. There is nothing I can do to increase His already proven love for me.

Whereas I used to wear the label of "bastard," Colossians talks about the fact that, in Christ, we are chosen, beloved and holy. Those are the new labels I now wear, and they establish my identity.

> ### *God says He chose me, and not as the last of the group.*

When I was a boy and the others would pick sides for a baseball game, it seemed everyone was chosen before me. It was as though I was a handicap to the team who chose me. But God says that He chose me, and not as the last of the group.

Recently I took my dad's hand and told him that there has never been a time when I loved him more or have been more proud of him than now. Tears came to his eyes and he said, "I never knew you cared. I never knew I was that important to you." He reached over and gave me a hug, and for the first time he said, "Son, I love you." How that penetrated the depths of my heart!

God is in the ministry of repairing our lives. He is changing us into His likeness, His image. He is putting all the pieces back together, touching all the relationships between father and son, husband and wife, parent and child. He has begun the good work and will continue it until we stand before Him, complete in Christ.

*   *   *

Where Is Your Identity?

There are a lot of sick ways to identify ourselves, and doing so by the color of our skin or the stigma connected to our birth are some of the sickest. If we had only a physical heritage, it would make sense that we get our identity from the natural world. But we have a spiritual heritage as well.

Paul repeatedly admonishes the church to put off the old man and put on the new man, "who is being renewed to a true knowledge according to the image of the One who created him—a renewal in which there is no distinction between Greek and Jew, circumcised and uncircumcised, barbarian, Scythian, slave, and freeman, but Christ is all, and in all" (Colossians 3:10,11). In other words, stop identifying yourself along racial, religious, cultural and social lines. Find your common identity in Christ!

Bondage to Sin

Anybody who would heap more condemnation on this pastor or anyone else who struggles in this way is assisting the devil, not God. The devil is the adversary; Jesus is our advocate. People trapped by sexual sin would love nothing more than to be free.

No pastor in his rational mind would throw away his ministry for a one night stand, and yet many do. Why is that? Can we be a bond servant of Christ and at the same time be in bondage to sin? Sadly, many who have been delivered out of the kingdom of darkness and into the kingdom of God's beloved Son are living as bond servants to both kingdoms. Even though we are no longer *in* the flesh because we are in Christ, we can still walk (live) *according to* the flesh if we choose to. And the first deed of the flesh listed in Galatians 5:19 is immorality (fornication).

I surveyed a seminary student body and found out that 60 percent were feeling convicted about their sexual morality. The other 40 percent were probably in various stages of denial. Every legitimate Christian would love to be sexually free. The problem is that sexual sins are so uniquely resistant to conventional treatment. Nevertheless, freedom is attainable. Let me establish a theological basis for freedom and then suggest some practical steps that we need to take.

Two Essentials

If I had to summarize the two essential functions that must take place in order for a believer to become free and stay free, I would say, "First, take action. Do something about the neutral disposition of your physical body by giving it to God. And second, win the battle for your mind by reprogramming it with the truth of God's Word." Paul summarized both in Romans 12:1,2:

> I urge you therefore, brethren, by the mercies of God,

to present your bodies a living, and holy sacrifice, accept-able to God, which is your spiritual service of worship. And do not be conformed to this world, but be transformed by the renewing of your mind, that you may prove what the will of God is, that which is good and acceptable and perfect.

In this chapter I want to address the issue of habitual sexual sin as it relates to the physical body. In the next chapter I will deal with the battle for our mind as it relates to sexual bondage.

In Romans 6:12, we are admonished not to let sin reign in our mortal body that we should obey its lusts. That's our responsibility: not to let sin rule in our members. The difficulty is that the source of the conflicts is "your pleasures that wage war in your members" (James 4:1).

Dead to Sin

In Romans 6:6,7, you'll find the basic understanding we need in order to *not* let sin reign in our bodies: "Knowing this, that our old self was crucified with Him, that our body of sin might be done away with, that we should no longer be slaves to sin; for he who has died is freed from sin." I often ask in a conference, "How many have died with Christ?" Everybody will raise their hands. Then I will ask, "How many are free from sin?" It had better be the same hands, or these people have a problem with Scripture.

When we fail in our Christian walk we often reason, "What experience must I have in order for me to live as though I have really died with Christ?" The only experience necessary was the experience that Christ had on the cross. Many try and try to put the old self (man) to death and can't. Why not? Because the old self has already died! You cannot do what has already been done for you by Christ. Most Christians are desperately trying to become what they already are. We receive Christ by faith . . . we walk by faith . . . we are justified by faith . . . and we are also sanctified by faith.

In my experience, however, I often don't feel dead to sin. I often *feel* alive to sin and dead to Christ, even though we are admonished to "consider yourselves to be dead to sin, but alive to God *in* Christ Jesus" (Romans 6:11). It is important to recognize that considering this to be so isn't what makes it so. We consider it so because it *is* so. Believing something doesn't make it true. It's true; therefore, I believe it. And when we choose to walk by faith according to what Scripture affirms is true, it works out in our experience. So to summarize: You can't die to sin because you have already died to sin. You choose to believe that truth and walk in it by faith, and then the result of being dead to sin works out in your experience.

In a similar fashion, I don't serve the Lord in order to gain His approval. I am approved by God; therefore, I serve Him. I don't try to live a righteous life in the hopes that some day He will love me. I live a righteous life because He already loves me. I don't labor in the vineyard trying to gain His acceptance. I am accepted in the beloved; therefore, I gladly serve Him.

Living Free

When sin makes its appeal, I say, "I don't have to sin because I have been delivered out of darkness and I am now alive in Christ. Satan, you have no relationship to me, and I am no longer under your authority." Sin hasn't died. It's still strong and appealing, but I am no longer under its authority and I have no relationship to the kingdom of darkness. Romans 8:1,2 helps to clarify the issue: "There is therefore now no condemnation for those who are in Christ Jesus. For the law of the Spirit of life in Christ Jesus has set you free from the law of sin and death."

Is the law of sin and death still operative? Yes, and it applies for everyone who isn't in Christ, those who have not received Him into their lives as Savior. It is also in effect for those who are Christians but who choose to live according to the flesh. In the natural world, we can fly if we overcome the law of gravity by a greater law. But the moment we disconnect that greater power we will lose altitude.

That's the way it is in our Christian life. The law of sin and death has been superseded by a higher power—the resurrection life of Christ. But we will fall the moment we stop walking in the Spirit and living by faith. So we need to "put on the Lord Jesus Christ, and make no provision for the flesh in regard to its lusts" (Romans 13:14). Satan can't do anything about our position in Christ, but if he can get us to believe it isn't true, we will live as though it's not, even though it is true.

Our Mortal Bodies

In Romans 6:12 we're told not to let sin reign in our mortal bodies, and then verse 13 gives insight on how to accomplish that: "Do not go on presenting the members of your body to sin as instruments of unrighteousness but present yourselves to God as those alive from the dead, and your members as instruments of righteousness to God." Our bodies are like an instrument that can be used for good or evil. They are not evil, but they are mortal, and whatever is mortal is corruptible.

But for the Christian, there is the wonderful anticipation of the resurrection when we shall receive an imperishable body like that of our Lord (1 Corinthians 15:35*ff*). Until then, we have a mortal body that can be used in the service of sin as an instrument of unrighteousness, or in the service of God as an instrument of righteousness.

Obviously, it's impossible to commit a sexual sin without using our body as an instrument of unrighteousness. When we do, we allow sin to reign in our mortal body and are being obedient to the lusts of the flesh instead of being obedient to God.

I personally believe that the word *sin* in Romans 6:12 is personified, referring to the person of Satan: "Therefore do not let sin reign in your mortal body that you should obey its lusts." Satan is sin: the epitome of evil, the prince of darkness, the father of lies. I would have a hard time understanding how only a principle (as opposed to an evil personal influence) would reign in my mortal body in such a way that I would have no control over it.

Even more difficult to understand is how I could get a principle out of my body. Paul says, "I find then the principle that *evil* is present in me, *the one* who wishes to do good"

(Romans 7:21). What is present in me is evil—the person, not the principle—and it is present in me because at some time I used my body as an instrument of unrighteousness.

Paul concludes with the victorious promise that we do not have to remain in that unrighteous state: "Who will set me free from the body of this death? Thanks be to God through Jesus Christ our Lord!" (Romans 7:24,25) Jesus will set us free!

Sinning With Our Bodies

First Corinthians 6:15-20 shows the vital connection between sexual sin and the use of our bodies:

> Do you not know that your bodies are members of Christ? Shall I then take away the members of Christ and make them members of a harlot? May it never be! Or do you not know that the one who joins himself to a harlot is one body with her? For He says, "The two shall become one flesh." But the one who joins himself to the Lord is one spirit with Him. Flee immorality [fornication]. Every other sin that a man commits is outside the body, but the immoral man sins against his own body. Or do you not know that your body is a temple of the Holy Spirit who is in you, whom you have from God, and that you are not your own? For you have been bought with a price: therefore glorify God in your body.

Every believer is in Christ and is a member of His body. For me to join my body with a harlot would be to use my body to sin, as opposed to using it as a member of Christ's body, the church. "Yet the body is not for immorality, but for the Lord; and the Lord is for the body" (1 Corinthians 6:13). If you are united to the Lord *in* Christ, can you imagine the inner turmoil that will result if you are at the same time united physically to a harlot? That union creates an unholy bond that is in opposition to the spiritual union that we have in Christ. The resulting bondage is so great that Paul warns us to "flee immorality." Run from it!

Sexual sins are in a category all by themselves, since every other sin is outside the body. We can be creative in how we arrange, organize or otherwise use what God has created, but we don't spontaneously create something out of nothing as only God can do. Procreation is the only creative act that the Creator allows man to participate in, and God provides careful instruction as to how we are to oversee the process of bringing life into this world. He confines sex to an intimate act of marriage, requires the marriage bond to last until death separates, and charges parents to provide a nurturing atmosphere where children can be brought up in the Lord.

Satanic Perversion

Anybody who has helped victims get out of Satanic ritual abuse knows how profoundly Satan violates God's standards. Those rituals are the most disgusting sexual orgies your mind would ever dare entertain. It isn't sex as a normal human would understand it. Instead it is the most ripping, obscene, violent exploitation of another human being you can imagine. Little children are raped and tortured. The Satanist's ultimate "high" is to sacrifice some innocent victim at the point of orgasm. The word "sick" doesn't do justice to the abuse. "Total wickedness" and "absolute evil" better epitomize the utter degradation of Satan and his legions of demons. If Satan appeared in our presence as he really is, I believe he would be 90 percent sex organ!

Satanists have certain breeders who are selected for the development of a Satanic "super" race whom, they say, will rule this world. Other breeders are required to bring their offspring or aborted fetuses for sacrifice. Satan will do everything he can to establish his kingdom while, at the same time, trying to pervert the offspring of God's people. No wonder sexual sins are so repugnant to God. Using our bodies as an instrument of unrighteousness permits Satan to reign in our mortal bodies. We have been bought with a price and we are to glorify God in our bodies. In other words, we are to manifest the presence of God in our lives as we bear fruit for His glory.

Homosexual Behavior

While homosexuality is a growing stronghold in our

culture, there is no such thing as a homosexual. Considering oneself to be a homosexual is to believe a lie because God created us male and female. There is only homosexual *behavior*, and usually that behavior was developed in early childhood and was reinforced by the father of lies. Every person I have counseled who struggles with homosexual tendencies has had a major spiritual stronghold—some area of life where Satan has control.

But I don't believe in a specific demon of homosexuality. That mentality would have us cast out the demon and then the person would be completely delivered from any further thoughts or problems. I know of no such cases, although I would not presume to limit God from performing such a miracle. However, I have helped many people bound in homosexuality to find their freedom in Christ, and steered them to a new identity in Him and to an understanding of how they can resist Satan in this area.

Those caught up in homosexual behavior struggle with a lifetime of bad relationships, dysfunctional homes and role confusions. Their emotions have been tied into their past and it takes time for them to establish a new identity in Christ. They will typically go through an arduous process of renewing their minds, thoughts and experiences. As they do, their emotions will eventually conform to the truth they have now come to believe.

Thundering from the pulpit that homosexuals are destined for hell will only drive the people who struggle into greater despair. Authoritarian parents who don't know how to love contribute to a child's wrong orientation, and judgmental messages reinforce an already damaged self-image.

Don't get me wrong. The Scriptures clearly condemn the practice of homosexuality as well as all other forms of fornication. But imagine what it must be like to suffer with homosexual feelings that you didn't ask for, and then hear that God condemns you for it. As a result, many want to believe that God created them that way, while militant homosexuals are trying to prove that their lifestyle is a legitimate alternative to heterosexuality and violently oppose conservative Christians who would say otherwise.

We must help those who struggle with homosexual tendencies to establish a new identity in Christ. Even secular counselors know that identity is a critical issue in recovery. How much greater is the Christian's potential to help these people since we have a gospel that sets us free from our past and establishes us in Christ! So as I counsel, I have people trapped by homosexuality profess their identity in Christ. I also have them renounce the lie that they are a homosexual and announce the truth that they are men and women. Some may not have immediate transformation, but their public declaration starts them on a path of truth that they can choose to continue.

The Path From Sexual Bondage

If you are in sexual bondage, what can you do? First, know that there is no condemnation for those who are in Christ Jesus. Putting yourself or others down is not going to resolve this bondage. Accusation is one of Satan's tactics. And most definitely, suicide is not God's means to set you free.

Second, get alone or with a trusted friend, and ask the Lord to reveal to your mind every time you used your body as an instrument of unrighteousness, including all sexual sins.

Third, verbally respond to each offense as it is recalled by saying, "I confess (whatever the sin was), and I renounce that use of my body." A pastor told me he spent three hours by himself one afternoon and was totally cleansed afterwards. Temptations still come, but the power has been broken. He is now able to say "no" to sin. If you think this process might take too long, try not doing it and see how long the rest of your life will seem as you drag on in defeat! Take a day, two days or a week if necessary.

Fourth, when you have finished confessing and renouncing, express the following: "I now commit myself to the Lord, and my body as an instrument of righteousness. I submit my body as a living and holy sacrifice to God. I command you, Satan, to leave my presence, and I ask You, Heavenly Father, to fill me with Your Holy Spirit." If you are married, also say, "For the purpose of sex, I reserve my body to be used only with my spouse according to 1 Corinthians 7:1-5."

Lastly, choose to believe the truth that you are alive in Christ and dead to sin. There will be many times when temptation will seem to be overwhelming, but you must declare your position in Christ at the moment you are first aware of danger. Say, with authority, that you no longer have to sin because you are in Christ. Then live by faith according to what God says is true.

Getting sin out of my body is half the battle. Renewing my mind is the other half. Sexual sins and pornographic viewing have a way of staying in the memory bank far longer than other images. Getting free is one thing; staying free is another. I will deal with that in response to the story in the next chapter.

7

Charles:
Freeing
the Abuser

I received a call from a pastor one day that started with, "Are you required by law to divulge confidential communication?" What he was really saying was, "If I came to see you, could I tell you that I am molesting my child or other children without being turned in to the authorities?" I reminded him that most states still protect clergy confidentiality, but do require licensed professionals and public officials, including teachers, to report any suspected abuse. I said that even though I'm not required to do it by the law in our state, I had a moral responsibility to protect another person in danger.

He took the chance anyway and shared his story with me. It all started with back rubs on his daughter to get her awake in the morning, but it soon led to inappropriate fondling, though no intercourse was ever attempted. "Neil," he said, "I didn't have a great battle with sexual temptation before this, but now as soon as I walk through the door of her room it is as though I have no control." When I talked with his daughter, I understood why.

What was happening reminded me of Homer's ninth century B.C. depiction of the sirens (sea nymphs) whose singing lured sailors to their death on rocky coasts. Every ship that sailed too close suffered the same disastrous end. In the story, Ulysses ties himself to the mast of the ship and orders the crew to wear ear plugs and ignore any pleas he might make. The mental torment of trying to resist the sirens' call was unbearable.

I'm not excusing this pastor, but there is a line in temptation which, when stepped over, will result in losing rational control. This pastor crossed that line when he stepped through the door of his daughter's room. As I learned later, the daughter had major spiritual problems stemming from having been molested by a youth pastor in a former ministry, and this abuse was never resolved spiritually. It wasn't the daughter who was actually sexually enticing this father; it was the demonic stronghold in her life. The "sirens" lured the father to do the unspeakable. When I met with the daughter, she couldn't even read through a prayer of commitment to stand against Satan and his attacks, which is a definite signal of enemy oppression. The father shared his struggle with his wife and, together, they sought the help they needed and worked toward resolution.

The story that follows is different from this in at least one respect. Charles's daughter had never been molested; she was never seductive and there was no apparent demonic stronghold in her life. But at some point in the pursuit of sexual gratification Charles crossed a line beyond which he lost control. His life became dominated by a power that led him to his daughter's bedroom and caused his world to disintegrate around him. Eventually he almost lost his life.

Charles is a successful professional who was abused as a child and who then became an abuser. Thankfully his story doesn't end there, for after the shipwreck there was recovery.

*   *   *

Charles's Story

God molds those He chooses.

My story is one of God's redemption and the freedom that comes from resting in His grace, a story of being chosen for His work in spite of the opposition of His adversary, Satan. As I write this, I marvel at how little of me and how much of God is revealed in what has happened. I can only praise Him for His transforming work.

I am free from bondage to a vicious assortment of sinful attitudes and habits that cost me the respect of my family, my co-workers and my church. This bondage had me on a relentless path of personal destruction that, if left unchecked, would have taken my life as well. This freedom was bought at a terrible price that I did not pay. The suffering, death and resurrection of my Lord Jesus Christ were what bought my freedom, not my own efforts or my suffering. The life I live is Christ's life, God's Son in me, not my own. And I rejoice that I am able with the help of the Holy Spirit to bring my emotions in line with what I know to be true about myself in Christ. However, this has not happened instantly, and the story of how God molds those He chooses is one of struggle and defeat as well as victory.

I ran for my life while my son
loaded his pistol.

"Put down your gun! Don't do it! Jesus, help me! Jesus, help me!" My wife's anguished screams echoed in my ears as I ran for my life while my son loaded his pistol, preparing to hunt me down and kill me. I reached my car in the driveway, fumbled with the keys (he's coming to shoot me!) and opened the car door. Throwing my briefcase into the car, I slid behind the wheel and started the engine. I backed out of the driveway and sped down the hill, leaving my wife to struggle with my enraged son, not knowing whether he might shoot her instead, not caring enough to stay and face his wrath.

I raced down the street imagining my son pursuing me in his car, ready to run me off the road and finish the job. The side streets beckoned as a way to evade pursuit; I made several turns, finally coming to a stop under a grove of trees. My pounding heart was so loud I was sure everyone in the quiet neighborhood could hear it. My shame was so immense that I thought the end of life as I had known it was imminent. I prayed, but all that would come out were groans and hot tears, and they were all for me. I had lost my family in an instant; I was sure my career, my freedom and perhaps my life would follow in rapid succession.

What had happened to me and to my family? What terrible fate had intervened in our affairs, threatening life itself? Where was God when I needed Him most? In my despair there were no answers, just questions and accusations. Thoughts of suicide fleetingly intruded, overcome quickly by my instinct for survival. After the initial fear of pursuit faded, I called a psychiatrist I had just met a couple of weeks before. Tearfully, I explained the situation.

I told my wife why our daughter was depressed; I had sexually molested her.

"Do you remember my telling you I felt depressed about my daughter being in the psychiatric ward for the last month?" I began. "She was committed for observation after she ran away and tried to commit suicide. Well, tonight I told my wife why our daughter was depressed; I had sexually molested her. While my wife was still reeling from the revelation, our adult son came in from work and she told him as he walked through the door. He became like a wild man, striking the walls, calling me a monster, and then he went for his gun. I ran for my life. When I left, my wife was struggling with him to keep him from shooting me. I don't know what happened after I left." I finished my confession and broke down and wept.

"Find yourself a place to set up housekeeping for a few days while we work this out," my counselor said. "Obviously, you can't go back there just now. And call me when you get settled in so we can talk."

Fear ran through me, unchecked, drenching me with sweat.

For hours I drove aimlessly, tortured by thoughts of

failure, of gross sin, of condemnation and rejection. I felt utterly dejected, despised by everyone—especially by God. I prayed and prayed but there was no answer. I phoned my supervisor at work, telling him I wouldn't be in the next day because of a family emergency. Then I started looking at rock-bottom motels which seemed to fit my current status. Each flea trap reminded me of how low my life had fallen, but my pride kept me from turning in to one of these and registering.

Finally I settled on a "respectable" motel, as if to deny the power of the events that had turned my world on its head. The desk clerk asked no questions, but I was sure that the disgust must have been lurking behind his calm facade. Once inside the room, fear ran through me, unchecked, drenching me with sweat. I had lost my family, my self-respect, my cockiness, and there was nothing to replace it. I sensed only anger, rejection, condemnation; there was no hint of hope. I prayed, weeping bitterly over my loss but not facing the sins that had led to this moment. I wanted to read the Bible, but it hadn't been included in the things I grabbed when I fled my home. The motel didn't have a Gideon Bible and I didn't think to ask the desk clerk.

Satan established beachheads in my life.

There was very little sleep for me that night. I kept waking, reliving the night before, trying to figure out what I had done wrong, how I could have protected myself better. I was focused on my own feelings of rejection and unworthiness, but not on my hurting family.

What events had led to such feelings of remorse and despair? Nothing mitigates the terrible fact that sin results from the decision to disobey God. You and I are both responsible for our own decisions and actions. Sometimes it's easier to learn from others' mistakes, though. Some background may be helpful in understanding how Satan established beachheads in my life through my responses to life situations.

I was the first child, followed by a brother and two sisters, in a non-religious family. My parents were married almost forty years until my father's premature death. Ours was a traditional family according to external appearances. My father held a succession of occupations but we didn't move very often, and material needs were always taken care of. In later years my parents were well-to-do and many luxuries were provided for us children. I felt loved and cared for (by the criteria I knew), but I really didn't know much about other kids' home life, so comparisons were infrequent. One of the characteristics of our family was that we didn't discuss how we got along, how the family was running, or our emotional response to anything. My siblings and I didn't discuss our personal lives with one another, much less with the outside world.

One of my earliest memories was of being spanked for having a toilet-training accident on the bathroom floor. Something I had regarded with childish amusement was suddenly transformed into a time of shaming, scolding and intense pain. I didn't know what I had done to call down such wrath; at that young age I was only aware of shame because I had disappointed my mother.

Someone had to be caught, blamed, shamed and punished in order for everyone else to feel worthwhile.

This episode was followed by many others in which accidents, careless or not, were met with punishment and shaming. Things didn't "just happen"; someone had to be caught, blamed, shamed and punished in order for everyone else in the family to feel worthwhile. I only recently learned that this pattern of attitudes had been passed down through both sides of the family for generations.

I was never sure I was valued for being myself. Value seemed to be placed on what I did. In our family we constantly jockeyed for position, trying to earn approval or denigrating someone else in order to look better by comparison. At a very early age I started to make choices based on how I would appear to my parents and any other authority figures who were in a position to judge me.

My parents were not religious. My dad, in particular, was actively hostile to all kinds of religion and rarely passed up a chance to make a disparaging remark about those who loved God. We never went to church (I was sent to Sunday school once, never to be repeated), and the Bible was not part of our family.

When I was a teenager, my grandfather gave me a Bible that his mother had given him. Its almost-new condition indicated that my grandfather couldn't have given me a tour through it after he gave it to me. He seemed to regard it as a kind of talisman to be passed from one generation to the other, but he never discussed its contents or his relationship to God (if any). So it sat on my shelf next to Bertrand Russell's *Why I Am Not a Christian*, and I got as much use out of it as my grandfather apparently had.

The spankings we got were brutal and inappropriate to the offense.

My father's career choices meant prolonged absences from home while he tried out new businesses in another country, leaving my mother to contend with raising us the best she could. When he was home, he was capricious and wrathful and the spankings we got were brutal and inappropriate to the offense. There was no warmth at any time, and I remember being told, "Get out of my sight! You make me sick!" on more than one occasion. My mother had her own emotional problems with my father and she was unable to communicate her emotions to anyone, much less her children. So we were on our own, coping in our unique ways with Dad's anger and rejection of us.

When I was about eleven or so I was introduced to masturbation by a classmate. Confused and fascinated, I found that I could feel better and have pleasure, if only for a few moments at a time. Lacking joy in my relationships, I found myself increasingly drawn to self-gratification as a way of getting solace and comfort when I was lonely or frightened or feeling rejected or inadequate.

The isolation bred by my solitary practice would have

been bad enough, but along the way I discovered the power of fantasy to enhance the experience and heighten the stimulation. Beginning with the lingerie illustrations in the Sears catalog at my grandmother's house, I soon found out about pornography through a copy of *Playboy* magazine that my grandmother bought me (thinking, I suppose, that it had something to do with giving young boys suggestions for play activities). When she saw the contents later that day, she quickly confiscated it. But not before my impressionable mind had its contents seared into my brain.

I learned to regard women as objects to satisfy my lust.

Finding my father's private stash of hard-core pornography on an upper shelf of his study gave further impetus to my lustful fantasies. He apparently had mail-ordered materials that were illegal at that time; similar items can be bought legally in neighborhood porno parlors in most communities today. I quickly learned to regard women as objects meant to satisfy my lust and stimulate me. Overwhelmed by the boundless promises of lust, I began attempting to make sexual contact with the girls my own age. I was rebuffed, learning very quickly that sexuality was something shameful. It was to be hidden, to be snickered at in locker rooms, but not to be discussed seriously with anyone.

I was adrift on the sea of lust, with no spiritual input and no sense of God's judgment at all. Each episode brought shame that could not be discussed with any friend, and certainly not with my parents. I felt more and more worthless. Throwing myself into academic pursuits, I became further alienated from my peers.

During all of this, I had the additional misfortune to be seduced by a man in a position of authority. He was a man whom I trusted and liked and whose prominence was such that I feared to tell anyone. Disgusted by the experience, confused by the attention and the sensuality, I felt violated but couldn't admit to my own rage about this until many years later. With my sexuality thoroughly confused, I continued to lust after any sensual experience I could read about or imagine. To satisfy my lust I seduced my younger brother for a period of several years, abusing his natural affections without compassion, pity or guilt.

Pornography became my escape from the pressure of social relationships and unpleasant responsibilities.

At the same time I continued to seek out other sensual experiences and pornography. I gravitated toward those that were heterosexual, but the more perversely sexuality was depicted, the more stimulated I became. The transient "adrenalin high" was mixed with shame, the fear of getting caught and the thrill of avoiding detection. The more I was involved with pornography, the easier it became to use it to relieve tension, escape the pressure of social relationships and avoid unpleasant responsibilities. Pictures on a printed page could promise thrills, ready acceptance, no conflicts—things that real women and girls my age couldn't offer. Each time I used the pornography I was driven into a depression that followed the exhilaration, and I swore that this was the last time. I reflected on what worthless scum I was. I became more and more isolated from people, rationalizing that if people really knew what I was like they wouldn't want any part of me.

After I began dating, my primary objective was to get the women I dated to meet what I perceived as being my sexual needs. Inflamed with passion by the pornography, I spent hours each day possessed by sexual thoughts and activities, missing assignments because of masturbation, fearful of reaching out socially for fear of rejection, and too stubborn to admit my life was out of control. There were interludes, of course, when my activities were more nearly "normal" because of involvement with organizations, studies and occasional "friends." Yet even these were kept away from the core of my being because I was afraid of exposure and rejection.

I could only think of more ways to indulge in evil.

Gradually I overcame my fear of girls enough to make a preoccupation out of seducing them and going as far sexually as I could. As this new outlet for my lust gained proficiency, my abuse of my brother slackened and stopped. I realize now the awful consequences for each of the victims of my lust. They were violated, their boundaries trespassed, their bodies used without care or respect. At the time I could only think of more ways to indulge in evil, each thought more perverse and against society's stand-ards than the last. Masturbation became such a preoc-cupation that my grades suffered and my social relationships eventually dried up. My constant search for stimulating fantasies and experiences hurt other people, invaded their privacy and drove them away.

When I met my wife-to-be, I was on the rebound from a sexually obsessive relationship that had no solid basis. Although I knew my new love was a Christian, I had only had fleeting contact with "Bible thumpers," as I called them. She was pretty, intelligent, caring and needed nur-turing; her childhood had been unhappy, too.

I didn't vow to be faithful, to honor or to cherish my wife.

I thought she would give up Christianity as soon as she learned the truth; she thought I would convert as soon as I heard the gospel. Neither of us received wise counsel against the relationship, much less the marriage, although we talked to several pastors before getting married. It was a hodgepodge of a ceremony. My bride read from 1 Corin-thians 13 and other Scripture passages, while I said nothing religious in my speaking parts and quoted from secular and mystical sources. Significantly, I didn't vow to be faithful or to honor or cherish my wife. At the time, I was very much "in love," but I hadn't the faintest idea about the commitment my bride was making to love me in the love of Christ.

Initially, my wife, in her eagerness to please her new husband, satisfied my lust. Even in the marriage bed I considered her just another object placed there for my pleasure, to make me feel adequate and loved. I didn't really look very hard for ways to enhance her pleasure, other than to order a copy of a Hindu treatise on sex that included hundreds of acrobatic activities that we weren't athletic enough to accomplish (much to my disappointment). I was still looking for the ultimate sexual high promised by the pornography but never delivered. Such notions as commitment, nurturing, caring, communication and fidelity were hard for me to understand.

After our first child was born, many bitter arguments ensued about the religious upbringing of our children. I insisted that they would have none. My wife tearfully shared her fear that they would be condemned to hell if they didn't know Jesus as their Lord. She wanted them to learn about Jesus while they were little. I was adamant that our children not be "brainwashed" but somehow learn about religion from someone else when they were adults. Although I took a course on the life of Christ and earned an "A," I still rejected the gospel. I was abusive, hostile and blasphemed the living God in my petulance and anger. Meanwhile, my life was in disorder, although I was the last to notice.

I accepted the gift of salvation freely offered by the Father through His Son, Jesus Christ.

Finally, in a time of crisis, having seen many responses to my wife's prayers that I couldn't explain away, I decided to accept the gift of salvation freely offered by the Father through His Son, Jesus Christ. I committed my life to follow Him, having very little idea what that commitment meant. For a time, I was so grateful at having been saved from hell that my lust was put on the back burner. But that didn't last long. I had privately renounced my past sins, but was unwilling to undergo the self-examination and cleansing that are necessary for a child of God to truly express the joy associated with following God in loving obedience.

When preachers or commentators talked about God as a "loving Father," that term seemed an oxymoron; I had not experienced such a father. I was expecting punishment, not praise. At the time, I didn't know what God had said about the matter: "Therefore judge nothing before the appointed time; wait till the Lord comes. He will bring to light what is hidden in darkness and will expose the motives of men's hearts. At that time each will receive his praise from God" (1 Corinthians 4:5, NIV).

Shortly after I became a Christian, I engaged in my first act of adultery. I had already had adulterous thoughts, but an opportunity to put my lust into practice presented itself, and I jumped (not fell) into sin. Afterward I was so ashamed that I didn't attempt to continue the relationship. I felt remorse and tried to pray, but I didn't acknowledge to myself or to God my full responsibility in the matter. Three more times over the next several years I took advantage of opportunities to have sexual contact with other women, and my involvement with pornography continued on an episodic basis, adding fuel to the fantasy life that detracted from my relationship with my wife.

I am responsible for my actions regardless of my circumstances.

Some misguided person might offer the "consolation" that perhaps my wife was unattractive physically or emotionally, and that somehow she drove me to these sins. I have two responses: First, my wife was (and is) very lovely, and during those times she was trying to be supportive; second, I am responsible for my actions regardless of the external circumstances. My focus on sex as the means for meeting my emotional needs led to decisions to demand or take that which was not properly mine.

As years passed, my wife began to be troubled by my increasing demands for unusual sex practices, those she considered kinky or perverted. At the same time, my occasional impotence or delay in climax became more frequent. We didn't talk about these things because my wife's occasional ventures into discussing sex were met with hostility, defensiveness or silence. I was so ashamed of the "rest" of my sex life that I felt it could not be discussed with anyone, including my wife. If anyone knew, my life would be over because I was uniquely sinful and worthy of condemnation or death.

I definitely didn't go to God; He only accepted those who were completely obedient to Him, at least in the "big things." I knew I was going to heaven, but I believed that God was only keeping a bargain. He couldn't really love me with the accretion of sinful things I had done. I felt out of control, powerless to stop my behavior. Even more serious brushes with the authorities didn't stop me from seeking the magical sexual "high" that would make me feel loved.

At the same time I pursued those fantasies, I was rejecting any real friendship or intimacy with my wife, with friends or within Christ's church. In our local church I was an elder, I led home Bible studies, I even pursued evangelism and saw several people accept the salvation of Christ after I had shared the gospel with them. But inside, I knew no peace.

I began to notice my daughter's maturation in an unhealthy way.

Some of the pornography I read was "Family Reading," a euphemism for stories about incest. At first the theme seemed repulsive; then it was stimulating like other perverted subjects. I didn't apply it to my own family at first. Then, as my daughter reached fourteen, I began to notice her maturation in an unhealthy way. My language at home became more suggestive, my remarks less appropriate, the jokes I brought home from work more sexual in content. I was less careful about modesty in my dress. When I saw my daughter in swimwear or nightwear, it became more difficult to avert my eyes.

Finally, when telling my daughter good-night in her

bedroom, I would find one pretext or another to "acciden-
tally" brush a hand against her breast, even while praying
with her. This happened over a period of several months.
I became afraid of what would happen next, but told myself
I couldn't help it, that I really loved my daughter. My
ambivalence interfered with my sex life with my wife, and
I found myself increasingly impotent with her. Even masturbation failed to satisfy.

One evening I offered to tell my daughter good-night.
"No, thanks, Daddy, I'm too tired," she said, as she went
into her bedroom and firmly closed the door. There were
no more good-nights after that. She didn't want me to hug
her or even touch her, claiming that her muscles were
tender from workouts. A gulf grew between us, but in my
deception I didn't attribute her rejection of me to the abuse
of our relationship, to violating her boundaries as a person,
to transgressing God's law. I attributed her coldness to
"growing pains," failing to recognize that I had hurt and
frightened her and had perverted our relationship.

I didn't confide in anyone what was going on in my secret life.

Several months later, relationships in our family had
deteriorated severely. No one was communicating effec-
tively with anyone else, and we were all barely coping with
day-to-day existence. After a thoroughly botched vacation
trip, with no one talking all the way back home, things
became even worse. My wife became severely depressed,
entering a psychiatric unit for more than a week. While
she was there we were all distraught, yet I did not confide
in anyone what was going on in my secret life that corrupted everything in our family.

Although I did not abuse our daughter during that
tumultuous period, I failed to take decisive action and she
became more depressed than ever. A couple of weeks after
my wife returned from the hospital, our daughter ran
away. When we finally tracked her down a few days later
in a nearby community, she was defiant and didn't want
to come back home. One of her acquaintances told us she

had narrowly been prevented from committing suicide. So our daughter went into the hospital for a month.

While she was in the hospital, not a hint of the story of her sexual abuse came out until the last week. In spite of repeated questioning by the mental health team and by my wife, she denied there was anything between us and so did I. It was as if we believed we could wish away the incidents, that nothing had really happened. But it had, and that monstrous sin festered beneath the surface, becoming more foul. There was little progress in our daughter's depression and anger, and daily my wife and I were becoming more distant from one another.

A compulsion to protect myself produced a protracted confession lasting four days.

Finally I woke up at four o'clock one Thursday morning, sitting bolt upright in bed with a compelling urge to confess everything to my wife. Although my intent was to tell everything, my almost-as-great compulsion to protect and defend myself produced a protracted confession lasting four days. There were falsehoods, half-truths, whole truths, all tumbling together with tears and remorse. She heard about the adultery, the incest with my siblings, my seduction by the older man, the confrontations with the authorities. And she kept asking about our daughter while I kept denying there was anything amiss.

Finally, on the fourth evening, I told my wife I had abused our daughter. She sat there in stunned silence and horror. "That explains a lot," she finally said. "I couldn't put things together in my mind, but now events make sense." Just then our son walked in and you know what the rest of that evening was like. A couple of elders from our church came over that night, prayed with my family, encouraged them as much as they could and offered their help. One of them took the guns from our house. My wife contacted the Child Protection Agency the next day (an essential action, mandated by law, when abuse is discovered).

I moved to a less-expensive motel for a couple of weeks

while my wife decided what to do. I couldn't call the house because my son was there. My days were spent in pain, grieving my losses, berating myself. I found a Bible and began reading verses about those who are in Christ and God's love for us. I cried a lot. I read Psalm 51, King David's confession of sin with Bathsheba, over and over. I prayed aloud to God; I screamed into my pillow and drenched it with tears. I wept over the remains of a wasted life, of broken relationships.

I began to realize slowly how my sins had produced consequences in the lives of others that couldn't be erased. I talked to our friends from church from my motel room, pouring out my anguish to them. I was amazed that they didn't hang up on me. They didn't approve of my behavior, but they were still talking to me.

---

*I knew I had to be with God's people,
even if they threw me out on my face.*

I couldn't attend the church my wife and daughter were attending, so I looked in the Yellow Pages for a church close to my motel. I was sure my shame was written all over my face, but I knew that I had to be with God's people, even if they threw me out on my face. The first service I attended was about sin and God's mercy. I sat there with tears blinding me, the lump in my throat preventing me from singing.

After the service I asked the man who had been sitting next to me to recommend a mature Christian I could talk to. Sensing the urgency in my voice, he introduced me to a man about my age who took me outside to talk. Sobbing, I told him the whole story, sparing nothing. "I didn't want your church just to accept me as some kind of super saint, welcoming me with open arms," I said. "I've hurt a lot of people and my sin has hurt me as well."

I'll never forget that man's response: "Friend, this church is a place for healing. You are welcome here." Unmerited grace flooded my heart and I wept uncontrollably at this generosity. I had never considered the church to have a ministry to people wounded by their sin.

But I returned the next Sunday and took the risk of meeting some of the elders of the church and the pastor and sharing my story with them. I asked for prayer for my family and for me. The response didn't excuse my sin, but made it clear that they considered me a child of God worthy of respect. I was overwhelmed by gratitude.

My wife was grief-stricken, angry, fearful and depressed over the revelations of my infidelity. In spite of that, she took time to call me at the motel and check on me. She got me the essentials for living out of the house and smuggled them to me. She spent hours in secluded places with me, talking out her frustrations and encouraging me to deal with reality as I confronted my sins.

We had periods when emotions were so high we didn't talk to one another for days at a time, but God always brought us back to each other.

> *"There are major problems here,*
> *but none that God can't handle."*

One of our friends from our old church recommended a Christian counselor he had known for years: "He's a gentle man, full of wisdom, and I've heard that everything he tells you he backs up with scriptural truths so you can check it out." Although I was seeing a secular psychiatrist, we decided to go to this man for help. He listened to the whole sordid story and said, "There are major problems here, but none that God can't handle." He began to teach us to communicate the feelings in our hearts with one another without killing one another's spirits in the process. He taught us the basis for sin and our reaction to it, beginning with Adam and Eve in the Garden of Eden and working from there through the Bible. We began to see hope.

In addition to the counseling sessions, our counselor recommended several books to read as we went along. One book he recommended was *Victory Over the Darkness* by Neil Anderson, a book about Christian maturity. For the first time, I began to understand that because I am in

Christ, certain things are true about me that are also true
of Christ.

Because of my identity in Christ, I have power over
the things in my life that I always assumed were beyond
my control. In particular, I learned that my emotions and
my actions are governed by who I believe myself to be. If I
believe a lie about my essential nature, whether it is from
the world, the flesh or the devil, then I will act according
to that belief. Similarly, if I choose to believe what God has
said about me, then I will govern my thoughts and my
actions that proceed from those thoughts in accordance
with God's will.

---

*I began to experience real periods
of joy for the first time.*

I experienced a dramatic sense of joy and freedom in
realizing the permanence and solidity of God's love for me
that transcends any particulars of sin. It was a profound
revelation to see from the Scriptures that I am not just "a
sinner saved by grace," but I am a saint who sins, one who
is called out and sanctified by God. I learned from our
counselor how to appropriate the truth that I have an
advocate before the Father who is constantly there to
counter the charges made by Satan against God's elect. I
began to experience periods of real joy for the first time,
interspersed with periods of melancholy and deep, abiding
sorrow before God for my sins against Him and against
other people, particularly my daughter and my wife.

Times of self-hatred were finally terminated by my wife
reminding me that, "You need to remember that if God has
forgiven your sins in Christ, you must now forgive yourself." I have had to work toward forgiveness of those who
hurt me in the past, not because those hurts are an excuse
for sins old or new, but because the unforgiveness kept me
bottled up. I have asked for and received forgiveness from
those family members I hurt (with the exception of my
children who are still struggling with it), and have been
reconciled to them, knowing true intimacy for the first time
in my life with my brother and sisters and mother. My

father died an unbeliever a number of years ago, rejecting the gospel till the last. It has been hardest forgiving him for the rage and neglect, but God has called me to that as well.

These groups could not offer the spiritual perspective that identified the life-changing power of Jesus.

I had been attending two different twelve-step groups for "sexual addiction," and finally quit when I realized that they were elevating sexual sobriety on a pedestal as the end of their efforts. Although they acknowledged a "Higher Authority," they weren't permitted to identify that Authority as Jesus Christ. And when they had a split vote on whether sex was permitted only in marriage or just in a "committed relationship," whether homosexual or heterosexual, I realized I was in the wrong place and left the groups for good.

The only thing those groups did for me was help me to realize a context for my sexual dysfunction in society: There are plenty of people out there involved in sexual sin. But these groups could not offer the spiritual perspective that identified the life-changing power of Jesus Christ inside the heart of those who trust and obey Him. Because of that, I am hesitant to recommend their "self-help" approach, particularly if it detracts from relationships within the body of Christ. These groups often claim in meetings that the "addicts" are the only ones who can understand one another, that they are the addict's true family. To a Christian, such an attitude misses the point of the body of Christ caring for its members who are hurting.

I learned how we enable Satan and his unholy angels to establish footholds.

The second book I read that shed tremendous light and was a pivotal work in giving hope and direction to my struggle was Neil Anderson's *The Bondage Breaker*. This book deals extensively with spiritual warfare and the demonic side of habitual sin. I learned how we enable Satan and his unholy angels to establish footholds, then strongholds in our spiritual lives as we fail to live in our identity with Christ and appropriate the aspects of His character that are already ours. In reminding me that Satan is a vanquished foe who has no power over me that I do not relinquish to him, the book gave hope for victory in the spiritual and the physical struggle over sin.

I began to read aloud the spiritual truths that Neil had included in both books that show our identity in Christ and the results of that identity. As I affirmed my identity and then struggled with the discrepancy between my attitudes, thought life and behavior, in contrast to my nature in Christ, I was often overwhelmed with grief and self-condemnation. I renounced the strongholds that Satan had established, experiencing progressive freedom as each trouble area was identified. It was only after months of struggle that I have gotten where God wants me: confident in Him, not in myself, and confident in His love for me that will not fade or fail.

My wife and I have worked for the last year toward re-establishing our relationship, based not on lust and exploitation but on the solid foundation of Jesus Christ. Gradually we have dealt with issues of sin and forgiveness, and we are friends again. We still have arguments, conflicts and hurt feelings to deal with, but our tools are better. We are building a track record of success in resolving our past and present conflicts.

---

*The bondage to sin that I allowed
to happen has been broken.*

I still struggle with my emotions, but I am able to feel the full range from profound sadness to great joy, and God is with me in all of them. Do I still sin? Surely, but I am a saint who occasionally sins, and I am able to confess to God, remembering 1 John 1:9: "If we confess our sins, he is faithful and just and will forgive us our sins and purify us from all unrighteousness" (NIV). And very importantly, I have been freed from the sexual compulsion that grew out of believing Satan's lies about my true nature.

With the help of my therapist I have been learning to recognize and acknowledge emotions. With the help of the Holy Spirit I have the power to will to do good rather than evil. I have not been magically freed from temptation: The more closely I draw toward God, the more the tempter presents opportunities for sin. Recognizing that my thoughts will bear fruit if they are allowed to, I constantly am making choices for what is right. The bondage to sin that I allowed to happen through my sinful choices has been broken. In the midst of the evil around me, I am learning to flee temptation, resist the devil and be in the world but not of it. I stand on God's promise:

> No temptation has seized you except what is common to man. And God is faithful; he will not let you be tempted beyond what you can bear. But when you are tempted, he will also provide a way out so that you can stand up under it (1 Corinthians 10:13, NIV).

I am learning to function as a person who takes responsibility for his actions.

Still, I am confident that God's timing and His methods are perfect, that His plan of redemption has no flaws. I am grateful for His restoration and I look forward to the time when all wounds are healed, all tears are wiped away and reconciliation in Christ is perfected. Until then, I am learning how to function as a person who takes responsibility for his actions, and I am learning to love my wife the way God intended. Now I am able to pray, to study Scripture with gratitude, to praise God for His grace, to rest in His provision for my life. Thanks to understanding my identity in Christ, I am free! I can live the life God calls me to live!

*   *   *

Who Are the Hurting?

Every spring I teach a class called "Church and Society," our basic class on ethics that tries to determine the church's role in society. In the second half of the semester we invite local experts to address specific moral issues. I enjoy the class because every spring it is a learning experience for me as well. As the guests come to give their presentations, I warn the students not to "pick up everybody's burden" or they will be overwhelmed. However, the concerns must be heard because these speakers are striving to meet the needs of hurting people in our society, and that is also the ministry of the church.

The continuous concern I hear from Christians who work with the abused in parachurch or secular agencies is their frustration with the church. They say the church is living in denial and actually harboring wife beaters, child abusers and alcoholics. That most often we fail to defend the victim and provide sanctuary for the abuser, under the disguise of not wanting scandal. Consequently, neither the abuser nor the abused get help. Their lives continue to go farther and farther off course as was the case with Charles.

Male and Female Sexuality

We are created as sexual beings: female vaginal lubrication and male erections take place in the first twenty-four hours after birth. Infants need to experience warmth and touch in order for parental bonding to take place, and trust is developed during the first few months of life. Abuse or neglect even during this time will have lasting detrimental effects, so it shouldn't be hard to see how severely a child can be affected if he is abused a little later in early childhood when there is even greater awareness. There is actually a sick organization of pedophiles that promotes incest, proclaiming, "Sex before eight or it's too late!" They seek to destroy normal sexual functioning even before it has a chance to develop.

All sexual anatomy is present at birth and becomes developed in early adolescence. Hormones start secreting three years before puberty. In the female, estrogen and progesterone are very irregular until a year after puberty when a regular rhythmic monthly pattern is established. The wall of the vagina thins and vaginal lubrication decreases after menopause, as hormone secretion decreases.

In the male, testosterone increases at puberty, reaches a maximum at twenty, decreases at forty, and becomes almost zero at eighty. Normal aging causes a slower erection and less sexual functioning, but not a complete stopping of those functions. While a man is sleeping he will experience an erection every eighty to ninety minutes.

All this is a part of God's wonderful creation which we are to watch over as good stewards. But as already noted, this beautiful plan for procreation and expression of love can be grossly distorted.

Healing Distorted Sexual Development

God intended sex to be for pleasure and procreation within the boundaries of marriage. But when sex becomes a "god," it is ugly, boring and enslaving. Heaping condemnation on those who are enslaved is ill-advised. Increasing shame and guilt will prove counterproductive and will not produce good mental health, Christian character or self-control. Guilt does not inhibit sexual arousal, and may even contribute to it and keep us from using our sexuality wholesomely as God intends. Instead of condemnation, I would offer the following steps for those who have had a distorted sexual development.

1. *Face up to your present condition before God.* There are no secrets with God. He knows the thoughts and intentions of your heart (Hebrews 4:11-13), and you don't ever have to fear rejection by being honest with Him and confessing your sin and need. Confession is simply being truthful with God and living in continuous agreement with Him. The opposite of confession is not silence but rationalization and self-justification, attempting to excuse or deny your problem. This will never lead you to freedom. Your journey out of sexual bondage must include God in an honest and intimate way.

2. *Commit yourself to a biblical view of sex.* All sexual expressions were intended by God to be associated with love

and trust which are necessary to insure good sexual functioning. Recent evidence indicates that trust may be one of the
most important factors determining orgasmic capacity in
women. To ensure trust means that we never have the right
to violate another person's conscience. *If it is wrong for your
spouse, it is wrong for you.*

Too many wives have tearfully asked me if they have to
submit to their husband's every request. Usually their husbands are asking for some kinky expression hoping to satisfy
their lust. Some actually appeal to Hebrews 13:4, saying the
"wedding bed is undefiled" and claiming that the Bible permits
all expressions of sex in a marriage. No four words are taken
out of context more than those. Finish the verse: "for for-
nicators and adulterers God will judge." The idea is to keep
the wedding bed undefiled with no adultery or fornication. A
wife can meet the sexual needs of her husband, but she will
never be able to satisfy his lust.

A biblical view of sex is always personal. It is an intimate
expression of two people who are in love with each other.
People who are in bondage to sex or are bored with it have
depersonalized it. They become obsessed with sexual
thoughts in hope for more excitement, and because obses-
sional sex is always depersonalized, boredom increases and
obsessive thoughts grow stronger. One man actually told me
that his practice of masturbation is not sinful because in his
fantasies the women have no heads! I told him that is precisely
what is wrong with what he is doing. Fantasizing another as a
sex object, as opposed to seeing them as a person created in
the image of God, is precisely the problem. And even the
porno queen is some mother's daughter, not just a piece of
meat.

A biblical view of sex is also associated with safety and
security. Outside of God's plan, fear and danger can also
cause sexual arousal. For instance, sneaking into a porno shop
will cause sexual arousal long before an actual sexual
stimulant is present. And voyeurism is very resistant to treatment because arousal is not just from the viewing—the act

violates a forbidden cultural standard. The emotional peak is heightened by the presence of fear and danger.

One man said he was into exciting sex. He would rent a motel room and commit adultery in the swimming pool where the possibility of being caught heightened the climax. Such people must separate fear and danger from sexual arousal. A biblical view of sex includes the concepts of safety and security so that the maximum fulfillment comes from a complete surrender of oneself to another in trust and love. Some people buy the lie that the forbidden fruit is the sweetest, denying the crucial importance of the relationship between a man and woman in finding pleasure and fulfillment in sex.

I also advocate abstaining from any use of the sex organs other than that which was intended by the Creator. I was not built upside down, nor intended to walk on my hands. Parts of my body are created to dispose of unusable body fluids and substances. I do not believe that oral sex reflects the Creator's design for proper use of body parts. Even personal hygiene would suggest that this expression isn't what God intended.

Why are we continually looking for the ultimate sexual experience? Why aren't we looking for the ultimate personal experience with God and each other, and letting sex within marriage be an expression of that? Good sex will not make a good marriage, but a good marriage will have good sex.

3. *Seek forgiveness from all those you have sexually offended.* I encourage every man to go to his wife and ask for forgiveness for any violation of trust. Our wives can sense when something is wrong; don't let them guess. They are actually a critical part of our living sexually free in Christ. Men are incredibly vulnerable sexually and need the caring support and discernment that a loving wife can provide. Both Doug, from our last chapter, and Charles finally confessed everything to their wives. Humbling? Yes, but that is the path to freedom.

Charles also had to seek forgiveness from his children. In some cases, it may take years before that comes. Sadly, some never come to the point of forgiving their abuser, and so the cycle of abuse continues. Abused children usually become abusive themselves, and their children will suffer the result of yet another parent in bondage. If the victim chooses not to forgive the abuser, he or she is living in the bondage of bitterness. Yet for the restored abuser to live in condemnation because he or she has not been forgiven by the victim is to deny the finished work of Christ. Christ died once for all for the sins of the world. We must believe, live and teach that in order to stop the cycle of abuse.

4. *Renew your mind.* Abnormal sex is a product of obsessive thoughts. These thoughts become self-perpetuating because of the physical and mental reinforcement that comes from each mental perception and repeated action. The mind can only reflect upon that which is seen, stored or vividly imagined, and we are responsible for what we think and for our own mental purity.

I remember when I first became a Christian and committed myself to clean up my mind. As you can imagine, the problem became worse, not better. If you are giving in to sexual thoughts, temptation doesn't seem that strong, but when you determine not to sin, temptation becomes stronger. I remember singing songs just to keep my mind focused. My life and experiences would be quite innocent compared to most people I have talked to, but it took years to renew my mind from the images I had programmed into it earlier.

Imagine your mind to be the coffee in a pot. The fluid is dark and smelly because of the old coffee grounds (pornographic material and sexual experiences) that have been put into it and left there. There is no way to rid the bitter taste and ugly coloring that now permeate it, no way to filter it out. You can, and must, get rid of the "grounds." All pornographic material must go!

Now imagine a bucket of crystal clear ice alongside the coffee pot. Each ice cube represents the Word of God. If we were to take at least one ice cube every day and put it into the coffee pot, the coffee would eventually be watered down to the point where you couldn't even smell or see the coffee that was originally in there. That would work, provided you also committed yourself not to put any more coffee grounds in the pot.

Paul writes in Colossians 3:15: "And let the peace of Christ rule in your hearts, to which indeed you were called in one body; and be thankful." How are we going to let Christ rule in our heart? The next verse says, "Let the word of Christ richly dwell within you, with all wisdom teaching and admonishing one another with psalms and hymns and spiritual songs, singing with thankfulness in your hearts to God."

Just like Jesus, we must stand against temptation with the truth of God's Word. When that tempting thought first hits, take it captive to the obedience of Christ (2 Corinthians 10:5). "How can a young man keep his way pure? By keeping it according to Thy word. Thy word I have treasured in my heart, that I may not sin against Thee" (Psalm 119:9,11).

Winning the battle for our minds is often two steps forward and one step back. Eventually, it is three steps forward and one back. Then it's five steps forward and one back, until there are so many positive steps forward that the "one back" is a fading memory. Remember, you may despair in asking God to forgive you when you fall again and again, but He never despairs in forgiving.

5. *Seek legitimate relationships that meet your needs of love and acceptance.* People with sexual addictions tend to isolate themselves. We need each other; we were never designed to survive alone. Charles sought out Christian help and fellowship. Few do that, however, because of the shame. Consequently, they stay in bondage. When we are satisfied in our relationships, deep legitimate needs are met. Finding fulfillment in sexual expressions instead of relationships will lead to addiction.

6. *Learn to walk by the Spirit.* Galatians 5:16 says, "Walk by the Spirit, and you will not carry out the desires of the flesh." A legalistic walk with God will only bring condemnation, but a dependent relationship with Him, with His grace sustaining us, is our real hope. In my book *Walking Through the Light*, I seek to define what it means to have God's guidance and a life that is enabled by His Spirit.

Admittedly, sexual bondage is a difficult bondage to break, but every person can be freed from Satan's grasp in that area. The terrible cost of not fighting for that freedom is too high a price to pay. Your sexual and spiritual freedom are worth the fight.

8

A Family:
Freed From
False Teachers

The most insecure people you will ever meet are control-lers. They are external, not internal, people; shallow, not deep. Subconsciously, they labor under the false belief that their self-worth is dependant upon controlling or manipulating the world around them. Consider the Hitlers and Husseins of the world. Their insecurities have gone to such extremes that the lives of millions have been lost. Controllers of this nature simply eliminate those who oppose them and surround them-selves with puppets who outwardly affirm them.

In a similar and sinister way, false prophets and teachers have crept into the church. We have been clearly warned about them in Scripture: "For false Christs and false prophets will arise and will show great signs and wonders, so as to mislead, if possible, even the elect" (Matthew 24:24). It still surprises me to learn that the followers of cultish-type leaders come from educated, middle-class and usually religious homes. Are we that susceptible to deception? Yes, we are!

In 2 Peter, we find the entire second chapter devoted to false prophets and teachers who will rise up, appearing to be Christian. Notice the first two verses:

> But false prophets also arose among the people, just as there will also be false teachers among you, who will

secretly introduce destructive heresies, even denying the Master who bought them, bringing swift destruction upon themselves. And many will follow their sensuality, and because of them the way of truth will be maligned.

The Sinister Side of Religious Deception

When the way of truth is maligned, the result is bondage instead of freedom. Who will follow such deceivers? Usually, dependant people and those who are products of controlling, manipulative parents. Some are idealists disillusioned by a promiscuous society.

Abuse by religious deception is even more sinister than the physical or sexual abuse we have been discussing because this masquerade comes with high commitment, noble-sounding ideas and rigid controls. Thus it destroys decent people who are looking to be led by someone they can trust. Without realizing it, they end up following a man, not God. Paul warns us in 2 Corinthians 11:13-15:

> For such men are false apostles, deceitful workers, disguising themselves as apostles of Christ. And no wonder, for even Satan disguises himself as an angel of light. Therefore it is not surprising if his servants also disguise themselves as servants of righteousness; whose end shall be according to their deeds.

Stifling Legalism

In *Walking Through the Darkness,* I discuss the nature of false prophets and teachers, and false guidance. Nothing is more repugnant to God than those who would lead His children astray. False teachers have an independent spirit; they won't answer to anyone. They will demand absolute allegiance to themselves and charge you with not being submissive if they don't receive it. Instead of liberating people in Christ they exercise rigid controls, often under the disguise of discipleship. They insist that they are right, everyone else is wrong, and their pawns can do nothing unless it is approved by them. The fruit of their spirit is leader-control, resulting in a stifling legalism. The fruit of the Holy Spirit is self-control, resulting in freedom.

God is holy and we are to live holy lives, but legalism is not the means by which we will be able to do so. External controls cannot accomplish what only the indwelling Holy Spirit can accomplish. Legalists are driven, compulsive people who are trying to live up to some standard and never able to do so. They even require others to try and ironically reject them when they can't. They live under the curse of condemnation: "For as many as are of the works of the Law are under a curse" (Galatians 3:10).

Legalists try to establish their sufficiency in themselves, not Christ:

> Not that we are adequate in ourselves to consider anything as coming from ourselves, but our adequacy is from God, who also made us adequate as servants of a new covenant, not of the letter, but of the Spirit; for the letter [of the law] kills, but the Spirit gives life (2 Corinthians 3:5,6).

> Now the Lord is the Spirit; and where the Spirit of the Lord is, there is liberty (2 Corinthians 3:17).

A Family, In and Out of Bondage

Our next story is of a family who, over a ten-year period of time, journeyed into and then out of bondage. When I met him, Joe was competent and successful in his profession, but his marriage was in jeopardy. His wife had gone away for a few days in order to contemplate separation from him. His eyes expressed his deep concern as he came to ask for counsel. We will hear first from this conscientious man who unwittingly led his family into the bondage of a cult leader disguised as a righteous mentor. Joe's great difficulty was to admit to the deception; once he had, he struggled with whom to trust next.

Then we will hear from his wife, who discerned that something was wrong but was charged with not being submissive. Finally we will hear from their two daughters who chaffed under this oppressive atmosphere. I will not comment after their testimonies because they say it all.

* * *

Joe's Story

*My mother did everything she could
to hold the family together.*

My parents divorced when I was very young. After that, I remember feeling more trauma at the death and separation from others that I loved. My mother did everything she could to hold the family together, but her own insecurity demonstrated itself in a need to control.

Mom and I were always very close, but looking back, I see that she pressured me in my decision making, and molded me into being a person who needed someone else to guide me. This has had a profoundly negative effect on my entire life. I still often go through a "hell" of indecision in trying to choose a course of action. And once I do make a decision, I find myself evaluating it over and over again.

I did well in high school and especially college, gaining second place in my major field upon graduation, and I was chosen for an all-star sports team composed of students from all the colleges on the eastern seaboard.

---

*Cynthia hated our legalistic church,
but I gave my life to it.*

Cynthia and I met at seventeen, when she came to our home as my sister's guest. She was pretty and had a sparkle in her eyes, and I was attracted to her. We fell in love, dated through the college years and married upon graduation. We attended church after we were married, but I didn't come to know the Lord in a personal way until about a year later; for Cynthia, it was several years later. We went to a very legalistic church which Cynthia hated, but I gave my life to it. As a result of my dedication, many people there told me I should go into the ministry.

We moved to another church where I also became extensively involved: leading worship, assisting the pastors, writing curriculum, leading in small groups. That's when I began to realize that my relationship with Cynthia was suffering. Finally I resigned from all "ministry" activities to focus entirely on my home and family.

We became acquainted with a couple from another church who modeled a good family life and really helped us in our relationship and in raising our young children. It was through them that we were introduced to the discipleship movement that eventually shattered our family. We attended a service at their church to hear the leader of the movement who was from another state. I responded to his message and listened to his tape series over and over again. I became convinced that we should become involved in this movement.

Cynthia found it difficult. When she listened to the tapes, she was filled with fear. Our church leaders were also opposed to our becoming involved. So I submitted to Cynthia and to our leaders for a period of two years until, finally, there was agreement that we would join the movement.

I look back and see now that Cynthia never did feel good about that decision; in effect, I simply wore her down. But at the time I believed I was waiting on God to act on our behalf and that He had removed the barriers to our going.

My perspective of my wife began to change.

We joined the new church and gradually my perspective of Cynthia began to change. In my new interpretation of authority and submission in the home, I began to view her resistance to me as rebellion against the Lord.

I was hungry toward God and excited by the vision of the movement and the answers I believed it had for the problems of the church and society today. I genuinely thought that the church needed order and discipline, and that God had brought about this work to accomplish that goal.

I moved into some major responsibilities in the movement, both legally and administratively. We sold our home in order to move closer to the church and gave the equity to the furtherance of the vision.

The discipleship leader was abusing his authority and manipulating people.

Looking back, I see that in that movement there was one man, the leader, who was abusing his position of authority and using, controlling and manipulating people. I was one who was responding to his leadership, but I did it in the firm belief that I was responding to the Lord.

The warning I missed all along was Cynthia's concern. She continued to hold back. I realize now that in her spirit she could feel things were wrong, but she couldn't explain them to me, and I probably wasn't ready to listen. I should have paid attention to the reservations she was feeling; they were a part of the God-given guidance which I ignored. Instead, I saw her resistance as self-protection and my responsibility as having to help her.

Finally we were asked to move to another state where I thought we would be able to be even more involved, but that never happened. I didn't know it then, but after we were there awhile, the leader was telling Cynthia things about me that were hurtful and divisive. At the same time, he was telling me that I couldn't lead my wife and was not fit to have responsibility in the church. I was set aside.

That all happened as I was questioning the legal affairs of the movement. I had seen a red flag, and when I spoke about my concerns to the leader he reacted in anger. He told me that I was touching things out of the sphere of my responsibility and had no right to interfere.

A big barrier grew bigger between Cynthia and me.

I spent the next five years agonizing before God, trying to respond to what I was being told were my "problems." Meanwhile, an even greater barrier grew between Cynthia and me. I felt that much of what God had called me to do was being blocked because she always resisted me, the leaders and God. This attitude was nurtured by the leader in ways that were so subtle I didn't realize what was going on.

Gradually I found it more and more difficult to respond to the leadership's teaching and challenges. Yet we were being taught to keep responding to God by submitting to their authority. It was a painful and confusing time for me, and I did not see the many warning signals that things were not right.

When Cynthia got the idea to spend time in a training school—a live-in discipleship experience for the whole family—I was elated. I saw this as a change in Cynthia and we agreed together to go.

The discipleship leader was exposed.

The following year the movement's leader was exposed publicly, both for his handling of the finances of the ministry and for abusing many of the women spiritually and sexually. Together with others from the group, Cynthia and I pieced the jigsaw puzzle of the movement together and saw a picture of control and manipulation by one man that is almost too complex and incredible to believe.

Everyone believed that they were the only ones being victimized, and that the "problem" in their own life was the reason they could not move on to new responsibilities. Much of the control of people was maintained by dividing husband and wife; Cynthia and I were a classic example of that. But when the leader was exposed, that powerful controlling influence over all of us was broken.

We left immediately and returned to our home state to start life over again. Great damage had been done to our family relationships, the most treasured part of my life. I had lost the ability to relate to my children, especially my older daughter who had been struggling for a long time in the same way that Cynthia had.

There was a lot of change needed. I had drunk deeply

of a wrong spirit, brought it into our home and modeled something that was fundamentally flawed. I acknowledged these things to my family but did not realize that this was only the start of a major journey, not the end of our problems.

> *I found clarity and freshness in the freedom in Christ it portrayed.*

A book was recommended to me: *The Bondage Breaker* by Dr. Neil Anderson. I found clarity and freshness in the freedom in Christ it portrayed. I purchased his first book, *Victory Over the Darkness*, which Neil had referred to as being important to our identity in Christ. I devoured both of the books, reading and rereading them, and marking them throughout. There was not one area of the Scriptures in these books that I had not studied in depth, yet Neil brought a fresh perspective to it all.

I recommended the books to Cynthia and began to seriously consider going to California, hoping to see Neil. Imagine my delight when I heard he was coming to our area within a few weeks to give a week-long seminar! Cynthia was not that interested and went away on a trip to evaluate our relationship, so I attended on my own. At the conference, I was referred to a Freedom in Christ staff couple in response to my request for counsel. When Cynthia returned, she agreed that we would go together to talk as long as it was with someone totally independent, someone who had not been influenced by my perspective of the situation or of her.

> *I began to see myself in a new light.*

I met with the husband while Cynthia met with his wife, each leading us through the Steps to Freedom. During that session, I began to see myself in a new light. I knew of my identity in Christ; I could have discussed the issues from a scriptural perspective. Yet I began to see that I had built up a strong wall around many locked-up emotions which I had held since childhood. I was not in touch with my own feelings, but related to God and others on a mind level only.

The walls I had built around me were a self-defense, a security system under the cover of spirituality: great personal discipline, consistent study of God's Word, regular quiet times with God; but still a system where I controlled as much as possible in order to hold myself together. I had spiritual pride in my ability to respond "correctly" to situations, to control or suppress my feelings and emotions, to do the right thing.

It was my own "goodness" that was blocking a sense of personal poverty and need of God. What I didn't know was the humility of being in need of God in a personal way day by day. I knew the right thing to do, always had the "right" answer and could always back it up scripturally, but I did it in my own power. This aggravated Cynthia; to her, I wasn't real.

I found it very hard to be wrong, especially in spiritual matters, and often would not listen to Cynthia. She was the one who was "out to lunch" and needed help. I was encouraged to stop insisting on being right, to be free to be wrong, and to let Cynthia help me.

I had, in effect, destroyed Cynthia.

I finally realized that I had, in effect, destroyed Cynthia. I had given myself to God's work and, more specifically, to the vision and call of our discipleship leader, disregarding my own wife. What kind of person could do that? I had idolized a man, needing his approval because of my own insecurity. I had not understood the wonderful approval and acceptance of God even though I could teach all about it.

Coming to this realization has been very difficult because I sincerely felt that everything I was doing was for God and had His approval.

> *Satan is a liar and deceiver and*
> *very subtle in his ways.*

It is still difficult for me to understand how, in my longing for God, I could have been so deceived by the enemy of our souls. The explanation, of course, is that Satan is a liar and a deceiver and very subtle in his ways. This ten-year experience has been a tremendous object lesson and it has left an indelible mark on my life and family.

Even after the Freedom in Christ seminar, I was still discovering more about the frightened person who had spent the past twenty years living for God while staying personally independent of Him — having spiritual knowledge, but living in emotional unreality.

Thank God I was able to face the truth about myself. The biggest barrier to the restoration of my family had been the need for me to realize my own sin. After asking forgiveness from the Lord and Cynthia, I spoke to the children, telling them something of what I was seeing about myself and how wrong I had been — that I was not a good reflection of what God is really like. We cannot eradicate the past, and we are far from perfect, but now we are on a new journey of grace together.

*   *   *

As Cynthia came into the lobby of the church, walking tentatively beside Joe, it was evident that here was a woman besieged by fear and disappointments. Her story follows . . .

Cynthia's Story

I used to cry myself to sleep at night.

There was conflict in my childhood home. While my parents bickered and fought in the living room, my sister and I held hands between our beds for comfort and cried ourselves to sleep.

I wanted peace so badly that when my dad became

angry, I would stay out of his way and try to keep everything cool and calm.

My dad was a proud worker who felt that a good man does a hard day's work, and he drank as hard as he worked. Basically, he had a tremendous work ethic which he imparted to me. I always wanted to do well and did so, because to do anything less was to let myself down. And I did achieve my scholastic goals, though I was terribly insecure within myself and unsure of my future.

Mom said that boys only wanted one thing.

During my teen years my mom bought all of my clothes at the second-hand store, and they were always too big. I had to take them in with safety pins. When I complained, Mom said that boys only wanted one thing and that if they could see the shape of my body it would give them ideas.

I withdrew from the kids at school out of embarrassment and just concentrated on my studies, especially English and imaginative writing. I enjoyed those courses because I could express myself through them. Once I wrote a paper on individuality out of the cry of my heart—a paper on being different but being accepted, being worthy in your own right even if you are different.

My friend said we would have a summer romance.

When I was a senior in high school, I went with a girl friend to visit a family in another city. I was stunned when my parents gave their permission because they were so incredibly protective of me. But then, my friend was the pastor's daughter. She had said that we would have a summer romance, though I was not sure what that meant.

There was another girl our age in the home where we stayed and she had a brother. I was afraid of boys, but Joe was kind, soft-spoken and a gentleman, just a few months older than I. Our friendship developed over the next few years and though I saw a tendency to control, I didn't recognize it as a problem that would pursue us.

Joe and I married, and for awhile I waited with excitement for him to come home at night. But I soon learned that he was a very insecure man.

I would cry every Sunday as we left the church.

His insecurity created serious relational problems when we joined a legalistic church. He was a seeking Christian and he loved the legalism. He was looking for someone who would simply tell him what to do so that he would feel secure in doing it. I would cry every Sunday as we left the church because they were always pointing the finger at you and telling you what you were doing wrong.

I got to the point where I didn't go to church. I didn't want to be like those people: downcast, unhappy, with no joy. The pastor even said that if you were a Christian and taught in a public school, you were as the heathen. A nurse working on Sunday was also condemned.

One time, however, I heard a visiting missionary speak. He laughed a lot and sang songs. I had never seen such a joyful Christian before. Everything I had tried before, joining the church or Bible study groups, had turned out to be emptiness, but that missionary became my friend and we began to meet with him for Bible study. One night the light went on in me, and I saw a loving Savior welcoming me and forgiving my sins. I received Him into my life and cried buckets of tears, saying, "I understand! I understand!"

I had a real fear that we were getting involved in a cult.

Then we joined another church, more legalistic than the first one. Joe was excited because the leader of a discipleship movement he was attracted to was a part of that church. He felt that this leader had the answers to the Christian life that he had been looking for. I felt just the opposite. I feared that we were getting involved in a cult; I had strong reservations about the teaching and methods of this group and about the leader himself. But Joe persisted and I followed.

Some of their teaching was that people should attend meetings, not only for long periods on Sundays but often throughout the week and again on Friday evenings. Children were supposed to be there at all times, so the young ones spent three to four nights in a row falling asleep on the floor. We were told that we needed "religion" removed from our thinking, so meetings were held at other than traditional times on Sunday. We were taught that the church was now our family, and we were to choose any meeting called by the leader over any family activity.

It was a steady program of indoctrination. If we didn't agree with anything the leader said or did, we had no right to come to him about it. Leaders were not accountable to their followers, their "sheep." They never had to apologize for any wrong done. However, sheep were supposed to be given what was called "the right of appeal" if they felt they had been wronged by subordinate leaders. In reality, this never happened. Sheep were always wrong and were taught that they were attacking "the throne of God" if they challenged or even questioned the leadership.

The leaders, or "shepherds," taught that they were above the sheep. They were not to befriend the sheep, but simply to make their needs known so the sheep could serve them. I never felt that the shepherds were supportive— their job was to point out my faults and errors.

My husband calmly told me that
I had a Jezebel spirit.

In the first few months of attending this church, I shared my concerns and questions with Joe. Unknown to me, he was relating all that I said to his shepherd. This was encouraged by the hierarchy, supposedly to help mature us. One day my husband calmly told me that I had a Jezebel spirit. Not knowing what that was, I asked him to explain. He said that I was a usurper, that his shepherd had come to that conclusion after hearing of my concerns. Joe was told that I was trying to run the home and was walking all over him.

For ten years, anything said or done in our home was judged by that perspective. Joe felt that he had no manhood if he couldn't lead his wife, and the church constantly reinforced that belief. He was told that he couldn't advance within the church until he had his house (me) in order.

When Joe and I had that first major conflict, I asked for a "right of appeal." We were given an appointment to see the leader. This shepherd told me that I wanted a "puppy dog" for a husband, someone who would follow me around. He also told me that there are many levels of maturity in the Christian faith and that I was only in the kindergarten.

I left the interview feeling that it had been unfair and that I had not been heard. The leader had tried to weaken my resolve and crush my spirit. Actually, he only raised more questions and concerns about the whole situation.

Unfortunately, as I became more wary, Joe became more enamored with the strong teaching and the leader himself, even writing long letters to the leader pledging himself as a bond servant to him. When I discovered this I was enraged—not only was my husband selling himself out to a man, but he was doing it at my expense.

I was seen as the enemy.

My husband had always been loving, kind and thoughtful, but that changed. He became suspicious, distrusting and resentful, seeing me as the enemy, the one who thwarted his plans.

Knowing his longing to find God and to walk in His ways only made this whole process more difficult. At this point we were encouraged to sell everything and move some thousands of miles to be near the leader who had moved the headquarters of the church to another state. This was like a sentence to me, but since I had no other hope for our marriage I agreed. With much anxiety, we made plans to move. Our two children did not want to leave home, school or friends, especially our older daughter. However, I was holding on to a thread that maybe this could be the answer and we could work things out.

"Be careful of Cynthia; she's trouble."

After the move, instead of finding help we were left alone with absolutely no personal contact for months. I found out later that the couple who were assigned as our shepherds had warned everyone with whom I became friendly, "Be careful of Cynthia; she's trouble. You mustn't spend too much time with her."

Joe was also ignored and even ostracized. Whereas he had been quite heavily involved in the legal aspects of the church for some years and had held significant responsibility in this area, he was now told that he was not even to ask questions or in any way become familiar with the workings of the movement.

I struggled. He struggled. Unfortunately, we didn't pull together. Joe still maintained that the leadership had to be right and became extremely angry with me whenever I voiced my concerns. Quite frankly, I couldn't see much of Jesus in what was going on. I had long since decided that if what my husband had was Christianity, then I didn't want to have anything to do with it. But then, I had been told I was in kindergarten spiritually while my husband was viewed as being mature, so I kept those thoughts to myself.

The children were taught that life isn't fair.

After some time in the new state, I suggested to Joe that maybe we should go to the training school operated by the discipleship movement. That decision was born of desperation and a belief that I did need more discipline in my life.

The rules for family behavior were very strict in the school, and our teenage daughter and Joe had many confrontations. The children were taught that their place was to listen, to obey and to have their will crossed so they would learn that life isn't fair. When Joe returned home from a trip, he would make a point of bringing a gift for only one of our children. It didn't matter if the same child was left out several times in a row—that only reinforced the lesson. This idea came directly from the leader himself.

Several months after graduating from the course, both Joe and I decided to return to our home at the end of the year. When we asked the leader for permission, he said that he didn't believe the Lord had finished with us yet and that he also had plans for us. But I didn't want his plans. Besides, the Lord had given me a Scripture personally, that "He had plans for me. Plans for welfare and not calamity, to give me a future and a hope" (Jeremiah 29:11). How I held on to that word.

As I studied Jeremiah the Lord gave me words about returning from exile. Joe, our children and I all felt we should return home and we were excited. For the first time in ten years, our family was in agreement.

The leader was asked to resign due to sexual impropriety.

Then a church meeting was called and the announcement was made that the leader had been asked to resign due to sexual impropriety with many women. The shock ran through the church, and then we absolutely knew what the Lord would have us do—go home!

Once home, the girls and I were euphoric, but Joe went into a deep depression that lasted for weeks. His belief system had been challenged. He was confused and angry and didn't know where to turn or from whom to seek counsel.

We were fighting again and we knew we needed help, someone we could talk to who was independent of the situation and who had a godly ministry. This was our cry.

Months went by, and Joe learned of Dr. Neil

Anderson's books, which he read with great interest. He purchased one, then another. Then he heard that Dr. Anderson was coming to town to conduct a seminar on "Resolving Personal and Spiritual Conflicts."

Joe was determined to go and asked me to come with him, but I refused. I did read the book he'd recommended, but I wasn't about to deal with ten years of abuse and control in a room full of people. Instead, I took a trip alone to another city to try to sort through my confusion and perhaps decide to leave Joe. I returned near the end of the conference, and each night Joe would come from the seminar and share a little of what he was learning. But I wasn't too interested—I had lost respect for him in spiritual matters.

I was looking for any suspicion of judgment or distrust toward me.

I did agree to meet with a couple from the Freedom in Christ staff near the end of the conference. I was scared. Too many times I had gone to talk to someone and hadn't been heard. When we walked into the church and met the smiling couple, I acknowledged their greeting but remained closed inside. I wasn't going to share a thing if I felt any suspicion of judgment or distrust toward me. I found none.

We had a brief prayer together and then the men moved to another room while the woman and I began to talk. She asked me to share my life and my hurts with her, and what transpired in the next couple of hours dramatically changed me.

I talked; how I talked. Realizing there was a receptive, sensitive spirit in this woman, my guard came down and all that had been locked in for those many years came pouring out. I felt for the first time in ten years that someone could hear me without judgment—just an openness and unselfish giving of time to let me release the burden of those years. Finally she took me through the Steps to Freedom, renouncing any and all contact or involvement with the cult.

*Forgiving God for allowing all of this
to happen was something
I hadn't considered.*

I was asked to list the names of all the people I needed to forgive. There were many. When I came to the former leader of the movement, I struggled—everything in me didn't want to forgive him for all he had done to devastate our lives. But I did. By an act of my will, I forgave him and a deep flood of emotion was released. Forgiving God for allowing all of this to happen was something I hadn't considered, but I realized that I did blame Him. Finally, I had to forgive myself for things I had and had not done through the years.

At the end I was tired and strangely humbled. I felt comforted by the fact that someone believed me, and cleansed because I had let go of the burden of unforgiveness. In talking about the leader of the movement afterward, I no longer experienced tightness in my chest and tension in my body; I knew I was free of him. My healing had begun!

*As a family, we have been given
hope and encouragement.*

My daughters agreed to accompany me, so I took them to the next conference that Neil was conducting. From the first evening, the girls relaxed and enjoyed the messages. They had spent many weeks at church seminars before and had come to hate them, but this was different. This man was real; he was even funny, and what he had to say made sense. Later in the week, both girls went through the same freeing process that I had gone through the previous week.

The changes in our daughter's lives have been profound. Our oldest daughter has a softness restored and her heart is so open to the Lord. The younger one released burdens of pain and unforgiveness. We are all free.

Joe and I still have much to work through. Daily

situations arise where we have to deal with old patterns of behavior. But I no longer feel it's too big for me to handle. We know that it will take time to walk out of the old way of thinking, but we are on the road to wholeness. We have hope!

*   *   *

Joe and Cynthia's oldest teenager, Judy, is an illustration of the domino effect which can take place when parents repent and communication between themselves and the children becomes real and honest. Here is the account of Judy's search for truth and her struggle with her own anger and rebellion.

Judy's Story

*I wondered how adults could ever
do anything wrong.*

When I was little I thought Mom and Dad were happy, but when I got to about ten I began to feel a lot of underlying tension. But that didn't matter—I still thought my parents were perfect and wondered how adults could ever do anything wrong.

Mom would cry a lot, and she and my dad argued behind closed doors, sometimes for hours and hours. I would lie in bed at night and hear it and not know what to do. It was frightening. Then Dad would come up and tell us good-night, but he wouldn't say anything else.

I became a Christian when I was very young. When I was a teenager, we went to another state and it was awful. The people there, and especially the kids my age, were so fickle. They were friendly on the outside, but it seemed their underlying motive was to hurt you and bring you down. I wasn't used to that and it took a while for me to toughen up. I would come home in tears because I couldn't handle the fact that people would gossip about me for no apparent reason.

It was as though the room was filled with evil.

I hated the church we went to and the pastor. When he walked into the room I felt like there was a dark presence there, as though the room was filled with evil. I would feel suffocated or claustrophobic and want to get out. I didn't like being near him at all.

When I went to church I withdrew inside myself. I didn't sing or join in the service. I just couldn't respond and that got me into a lot of trouble. My parents would say, "What's wrong with you? You're fine before church and you're fine after church. What happens?" And I didn't know what to tell them; I just didn't want to be there.

I must have been feeling all of the wrong that was there. I felt that the whole movement was fake. The leaders would stand up and yell to the point where it would hurt your ears, and what they said didn't make sense to me. It was all theology and a lot of words that weren't helpful.

We had to go to youth meetings; we didn't have a choice. If you didn't go you were frowned upon as a rebel and a backslider. The good thing about it was that I would get to see my friends and that was one of the only times we saw each other.

They wanted to know things so they could lord it over you.

In the authority structure, the big word was *framework*. It was all rules, very legalistic. From the top down, everything was the law and it affected me a lot.

The leaders were supposed to know everything about everybody. That wasn't so true of us because we were at the bottom level, but the higher up you were, the more you would know about everyone else. That was the power structure. They wanted to know things so they could lord it over you. It was my dad's responsibility to tell them everything about us.

We were constantly at each other's throats.

When I was fourteen and my parents were in the training school, there were really strict rules. My dad was in favor of all of them, so he followed them all the way. I was under pressure all the time and eventually I rebelled against it. I fought a lot with my dad, and we were constantly at each other's throats. It got to the point where, during the last year we were away from our home, I hated him with every ounce of me. Everything he stood for, I was against. I knew that I shouldn't be that way, but I didn't feel bad about it.

My mother would share some of the difficult things she was experiencing and I would talk to her about what I was feeling, mostly the pressure from my dad. Whatever I would say, he took as criticism; he always thought I was pulling him down, even if it was just a little comment.

I didn't trust my dad. One time I told him something and he went straight to my teacher and told her. Then my teacher came and talked to me. I couldn't believe it. I had told something that was very important to me and now it was being held against me.

Sometimes my mother would say, "There's hope; there's hope. He's changing; he's changing." But I would say, "I can't see it."

I didn't want to do anything that would make me a hypocrite.

When we came back home, my spiritual life was almost nonexistent. I wasn't purposely trying to turn my back on the Lord, but I made a conscious decision not to get into anything like we had been in. I didn't want to be a hypocrite.

When my dad started talking about the Freedom in Christ conference, I didn't want to have anything to do with it. He kept pushing and pushing, but we had been to so many conferences. We had attended teaching sessions where there were meetings every night of the week, and we had religion shoved down our throats. We had to go to those and it was awful, so I thought, *Here we go again.*

Dad said that he wouldn't make us go, but that he would really like it if we did. I don't know why, but this time he didn't seem to be insisting like he used to, and we were at a point where we were getting along a little better. But my mom, sister and I declined, so Dad went and just kept telling us how good it was. I thought, *Great, there's going to be some big changes here,* but nothing visible happened. Then Mom and Dad went to the counseling session together.

Mom's experience really hit me hard, and the two of us cried together.

The next day my mother and I went out alone. We talked together for hours. She explained what had gone on at her counseling session, and the two of us cried together.

Mom told me about the couple she had met with who were not judgmental. I thought I would give that a try. We went to the next conference they were at and I loved it. All the sessions were enjoyable and refreshing—no legalism. And the speaker was funny. He didn't talk at you, but would give examples from his own life and family. You felt like he was coming alongside and saying, "Look, I'm a person too, and I also have problems."

I decided to see the same counselor Mom had, and when I did I gave up a whole lot of resentment by my own choice. It was something I had to do. Now I pray for those people from my past.

Over the years there have been those times when I have had big, dramatic encounters with the Lord. But it never lasted, except maybe for a week or two. They were emotional, physical experiences with shaking and everything. There were good things, but there was also a lot of hype. Then I would be back to what I was before. It was always external; I wanted more. I wanted something deep that was going to last, and that's what this was. Something happened in me, and I feel different, definitely softer toward the Lord. I talk to Him and I feel content and peaceful. I'm happy. I'm really happy!

I now have a lot of respect for my dad.
He said he was wrong.

Our family still has problems, but we have an answer. Recently we had a disagreement and Dad got angry and withdrew, but the next day he apologized. He said he was still working through some things, and I have a lot of respect for him for doing that. He said he was wrong and accepted responsibility for what happened. Now we can go on because things aren't being pushed under the rug.

* * *

Joan, the youngest teen in this family, expresses her fear and finally her hope as the family reunites in Christ. These two girls are above average in intelligence, looks and personality. Their response to their parents' choices to forgive and restore are proof that one of the greatest gifts you can give your child is to love your spouse.

Joan's Story

Our parents were fighting more and
more, and I was really scared.

Before we left our home there was a time when I felt that Mom wasn't a Christian. I hadn't seen her pray and she wasn't participating in everything Dad did.

I loved doing things with my dad and believed everything he said. But when my sister and I began to observe our parents fighting more and more, I became really scared. Sometimes I thought they might be breaking up.

I became depressed and really didn't know what to believe. I just went off by myself. I would actually hide from people. If I heard footsteps, I would hide around the corner so I wouldn't be seen. And I really got into books. If someone wanted to talk to me, I would avoid that person by burying myself in the books and play-acting the stories in my mind. What was happening in my family frightened me, and this was my escape.

I wondered why God wasn't talking to me.

I thought everything was my fault, and I wondered why God wasn't talking to me. Why couldn't I be happy like everyone else seemed to be? My dad helped me accept Christ into my heart when I was four years old, but now I was having questions about Him and whether anything had really happened.

When we moved to the other state, I hated going to church, but thought that when I got older maybe I would understand. Sunday was supposed to be the best day, but it was the worst day of the week for me. It was so boring to sit for so long, not understanding, not being able to do anything. We weren't even allowed to yawn.

One time I was so tired that I did yawn. Dad took me outside and told me not to yawn again or he would spank me. I did it again and he took me out to the car, but didn't spank me when I told him it was because I was so tired. I was confused when he did that. Now I understand that he did it because he was told to. He was supposed to be in control and if his children made any disturbance he was supposed to punish them for it. It was the father's role to discipline and be in charge of the family.

I would hide from my parents. I was scared of talking to them.

When we moved back to our home, I was in bad shape. I would hide from my parents. I was scared of talking to them. School was frightening. I didn't have friends, and when the kids were unkind I didn't defend myself. I thought I was supposed to have grace and not get angry, that it was the Christian thing to just take it and take it and take it. I was blaming myself for everything that was wrong in my life.

Satan had a real hold on me with fear. When I learned how to rebuke him, things really changed. Now, whenever I hear thoughts that I know are not true, I say, "Satan, I rebuke you. Get behind me," and he goes.

Before I learned about my freedom in Christ, I was really depressed a lot of the time and avoided handling my problems. Now I am learning how to face them. I know the Lord is with me, I call on Him for help, and I talk to Him. He's my friend!

9

The Church: Helping People to Freedom

In December 1989, I participated in a "Power Evangelism Symposium." Only seminary professors who were teaching something related to spiritual warfare were invited. The papers that were read in this formal conference resulted in the book *Wrestling With Dark Angels.* All participants were biblically conservative, but they represented a broad theological perspective. My paper was the last to be presented.

Before I read my paper, I said, "I don't see the battle as a power encounter, but rather a truth encounter. I believe that it is truth that sets us free. Secondly, I'm afraid that in the past we've adopted a method out of the Gospels instead of the Epistles."

There is no instruction in the Epistles to cast out a demon, but there is much instruction for individuals to assume their own responsibility to get and stay free. Prior to the cross, God's people were not redeemed and Satan was not defeated, so it would take a specially endowed authority agent to cast out a demon, such as Christ or the apostles (Luke 9:1). After the cross, Satan is defeated, and every child of God has the authority to resist the devil since we are in Christ and seated with Him in the heavenlies. The responsibility has shifted from the outside agent to the individual. We have a very definitive passage in 2 Timothy 2:24-26:

And the Lord's bondservant must not be quarrelsome, but be kind to all, able to teach, patient when wronged, with gentleness correcting those who are in opposition, if perhaps God may grant them repentance leading to the knowledge of the truth, and they may come to their senses and escape from the snare of the devil, having been held captive by him to do his will.

Not Power, but Truth

The ministry God has given the church is not a power model, but is better seen as a kind, "able-to-teach" model that is utterly dependent upon God to grant the repentance. We can't set anybody free, but we can facilitate the process if we are the Lord's bond servant, know the truth, and can relate it with compassion and patience.

After I presented my paper at the symposium, I was asked if the truth encounter method works. I assured the friend who asked that it does because truth always works and God is the deliverer. He came to set us free (Galatians 5:1). I have seen hundreds find freedom in Christ in personal counseling and thousands in conferences.

Then I was asked if the deliverance lasts. It will always last longer if the counselees assume their own responsibility and make the decisions, rather than my doing it for them. It is the counselee who has the responsibility to forgive, renounce, confess, resist, etc. We, as pastor-counselors, can't do that for them.

Then I was asked if it is transferable. Truth is always transferable, but if we are basing our method on giftedness or an office of the church, then it isn't. Most pastors don't care to get into a power encounter, and some counselors would probably lose their license or get sued if they did. I advocate a quiet, controlled means of helping to free people—one that is dependent upon God and not some special person. It's not "Neil's method." It is simply God working through the truth of His Word to release people. Thousands of pastors and lay men and women around the world are using the Steps to Freedom to do just that.

A Transferable Ministry

One pastor attended a doctor of ministry class that I taught, and within one year he and his associate had led more than a hundred people in their evangelical church through the Steps to Freedom. When I spoke in their church, I was overwhelmed with the spirit of worship and the "aliveness" I sensed there. Many of those people came to me and expressed their gratitude to God. They shared how thankful they were to have pastors who could help them resolve their problems. The pastoral staff is now in the process of training others from their church to lead people to freedom in Christ.

In this chapter you will hear from John Simms, a godly Pentecostal pastor who recognized the need for deliverance but grew tired of the marathon power encounter sessions. He was also frustrated with his lack of "tools" to help a couple in his church who were in great need of his help. Then you will hear from the couple themselves who were taken to a fellow pastor, one of my former students, who freely gave of himself to guide them through the process.

I share their stories with you in order to convey that what we are sharing is transferable. Pastors can and must get involved in helping people like the couple in this story. And I believe that what we are sharing isn't an evangelical or charismatic issue, nor is it a dispensational or covenant theological issue. It's not even a Protestant or Catholic issue. It's a Christian issue, centered in the truth of God's Word, part of the eternal purpose of God.

* * *

Pastor Simms's Story

I'm just a pastor who loves people.

Pat and her husband, George, started coming to our church through the invitation of Pat's brother and sister-in-law. From the very beginning I knew that Pat had problems: She found it hard to sit in church, was always squirming, and would often just get up and leave. There was never any eye contact, and she was extremely quiet and withdrawn into herself.

It took awhile for her to gain enough trust to begin to confide in me and ask for help. I told her I'm not a trained counselor, just a pastor who loves people and is willing to listen and pray with them. I agreed to meet with her.

Pat came to our house and began to share the story of her life with my wife and me. I try to limit appointments to an hour, but she would often become so emotional that they would easily stretch to a couple of hours or more. I worked with her every week or two, desperately trying to help free her from life-long struggles with rejection, depression and pain.

Pat had blocked out a lot of her memory because of her hurt and unforgiveness. I tried to keep her focused on Jesus and the Word of God. I told her that she was like a runner with many hurdles in front of her. She would knock down some of the hurdles, jump over others, and some would seem just too big to jump over—but Jesus was at the end of the race. That started a long journey over a period of at least a year and a half, meeting at an average of every other week.

It was wearing to have someone that emotionally dependent on me.

Pat was always in need and became dependent on me, so I had to be blunt and forthright with her and keep turning her back to dependency on Christ and her husband. She accepted it well, but she still would call me constantly, sometimes three or four or five times a week. It was very wearing to have someone that emotionally dependent on me. I prayed about this all the time, wanting to do the best I could as a pastor but having responsibility to other people in my congregation too. However, she was one of the more hurting people that I was aware of at that time. Satan had such a stronghold in her mind that it was easy for her to be deceived. She often felt that I was mad at her, and I was constantly having to convince her that I wasn't angry.

I worked mainly with Pat, but would occasionally take George aside to talk about her needs and his as well. At that time, though, I wasn't yet aware of all that had been going on in his life.

It was in the midst of this ongoing counseling that God led me into contact with Freedom in Christ Ministries, a ministry I had never heard of before.

I wasn't looking for demons under every bush.

That contact with Freedom in Christ was significant because about eight years ago, when I was an associate pastor in another church, the Holy Spirit impressed upon me that God would use me in a deliverance ministry. That very day, two demonized people came across my pathway seeking deliverance and help. I wasn't looking for demons under every bush and had not even read any books on the subject, so I wasn't programmed to give that kind of help.

The first year I got every basket case around. One lady manifested demonic activity in my office and God graciously delivered her, but there was such a distaste in my heart for the laborious, all-night marathon of the deliverance ministry. After about a year I was ready to give it all up and just preach the Scriptures. I didn't want anything to do with deliverance anymore. It just didn't seem like there was enough power. I prayed, "Lord, I can't imagine You laboring all night with people. You spoke and people were healed instantaneously, and that's what I long for, what I want to see."

I saw that deliverance was much broader than I had thought.

It was then that I attended a ministerial meeting where Dr. Neil Anderson spoke in preparation for an upcoming "Resolving Personal and Spiritual Conflicts" conference. As he shared, I was pricked in my heart. I saw that there was something more I needed to learn, that deliverance was much broader than I had thought, and it excited me. I went home and told my wife, "This guy has really got something, and I'd like to know more about it."

About the same time, God brought a very tormented young man into my life. There were terrible things that happened in Frank's life that he had never told anybody. He had more compulsive habits and behaviors than anyone I had ever known and was diagnosed as schizophrenic and manic-depressive.

I knew Frank needed deliverance, so I took him to a couple of pastor friends of mine and we had several long sessions with him, trying to cast out demons. There were some definite manifestations, but he didn't get free and my heart just yearned for him to be free.

By then his dad was ready to ship him anywhere in the world for a spiritual cure. He gave me the name of a man who might be able to help, and my wife spent five hours on the phone trying to track him down. When I came home that night, my wife said, "You're never going to believe this. I didn't locate that man, but guess who I was put in touch with?" And then she told me that she had been directed to Dr. Anderson's office, the very same person I had heard at the ministerial meeting.

Pat couldn't go through the final session.

My wife and I, Frank's parents and Pat all attended Neil's conference. Frank was hospitalized and unable to go. The first part of the week was wonderful teaching about our acceptance as God's children. But when we came to the final session when Neil took everyone through the Steps to Freedom, Pat got up and left the meeting. She hit a wall at the forgiveness issue. She just couldn't forgive, and became emotionally and physically upset. Dr. Anderson said that some might not be able to resolve their conflicts in a group setting and would have to go through the steps another time.

I pursued this with Pat. I told her I'd heard about a

pastor in a nearby town who had studied under Dr. Anderson and who was helping people through the Steps to Freedom. I offered to contact him. She was fearful and torn, wanting to do it and then not wanting to. The voices she had been hearing had become "friends" to her and she was afraid to expose her past and problems to a stranger, but since I had become her trusted friend she did let me make the appointment.

How could she get free so quickly?

Pat's appointment lasted almost four hours. I didn't do much except be there for prayer support. A couple of times she almost got up and left, but the pastor coached her through the steps. When we walked out of the office she was smiling and happy. I was almost in unbelief. How could she get free so quickly when I had dealt with her all those months and there had been no resolution? But I knew God had used everything that had gone before to get Pat to this place.

My wife, however, was more skeptical. I guess she had sat in on too many of the long and tiring counseling sessions with Pat for her to believe a healing could come so instantaneously after our months of counseling effort had failed. That skepticism was short-lived. The women from our church went to a retreat and Pat went with them. After that weekend my wife came back and said, "I can't believe Pat. She is an absolute miracle." And that's really the best way to describe what happened in her life.

Pat began worshipping the Lord in our services and clapping her hands during the singing. She got free and she has remained free. As with anyone, there are times of little discouragements and defeat, but Satan doesn't have that stronghold on her mind; she has been loosed from that oppression.

Her husband George also found freedom over sexual spirits by going through the steps with that same pastor.

Frank's parents hoped this would be an answer to his problem as well. Unfortunately, Frank is not coherent enough just now to walk through all this and know what he is doing, but his parents were freed from some things in their own lives and we continue to pray for Frank.

God has brought a new understanding of deliverance to me. I see that it is a broader picture. We are so narrow-minded at times that we don't see that it's not just deliverance—it's the need to know who we are in Christ and what our authority and resources are to stand strong against the enemy. Included in that is the necessity of forgiveness. I think an unwillingness to forgive ourselves and others is the big issue that keeps so many in bondage.

* * *

We have seen a glimpse into the lives of Pat and George, and the results of a faithful pastor's efforts to help a very needy member of his church. Now let's look at Pat's story in depth.

Pat's Story

Our family never shared our feelings.

I remember things that happened at school during my childhood but not very many from my home life, except for some flashbacks that came during my counseling. Our family never shared our feelings and no one seemed to care about what was happening in each other's lives.

From the time I was four until I was six, my dad molested me sexually. Finally I told my mom, "I'm afraid of Daddy. He's hurting me." I heard them arguing that night and after that my mom stopped talking to me. She was angry at me and cut my long hair into a boy's cut. I knew then not to tell my mom or dad my problems.

The neighbor boy raped me when I was eight. I was confused, depressed and angry a lot of the time, and afraid of rejection. I never had a lot of friends and didn't like life. In grade school, I cut my hands with glass, feeling that I was a horrible person and needed to be punished.

If I thought life had been hard while I was younger, it became worse in high school. I felt as though I was at the end of everything. I could never drink enough alcohol to stop the pain I was feeling and the voices I was hearing.

But I tried. I drank before school, during school and on weekends, just to get through the days. When I finally got my own room at home, that became my refuge and I spent a lot of time there. It was a place to be away from my grandmother who lived with us and didn't like me.

When I was fifteen I took a handful of my mom's pain pills. Thinking about that and planning to do it was the most peaceful time of my non-Christian life. I waited until everyone was in bed and gulped them down, but I didn't take enough and just slept all the next day. My mom didn't say anything about it and sent me off to school the day after that. I cried in all my classes, and finally my teacher called my mom and asked her to pick me up. She took me to the doctor, and he directed us to a psychiatrist who put me on anti-depressants and began regular counseling with me.

One day when my dad picked me up after a counseling appointment, I had a strange feeling—as if he were another person. His eyes had an evil expression as they did when he used to abuse me. I think he was afraid that I would expose him to my doctor. I tried to overdose two more times after that.

"The only thing that's going to help you is not going to be me."

While I was still in high school I got a job as a waitress at a Christian conference center. I think I got it by lying on the application about my experience with God. One day I talked with another waitress about my problems and she introduced me to George. I'd heard he was a "Jesus person." I really didn't know what to think about someone who talked about Jesus all the time, but he was nice and kind of cute.

As I got to know him, I really appreciated how he listened to me and tried to help. Then one starlit December night we were standing in the parking lot after work, and he said, "Pat, we can talk and talk and talk, but the only thing that is going to help you in your life is not going to be me. It's going to be the Lord." That's when, at the age of seventeen, I invited Christ into my life.

My life changed then, as though a big pressure and heaviness was released from inside of me. I hungered to read my Bible and it didn't bother me that my mom thought it was just a phase I was going through.

I was grateful to George for leading me to Christ. We began dating and later he asked me to marry him. When we told my mother about our plans, her response to George was, "Don't get her pregnant. I don't want another bastard in the family." She had been pregnant before she married, and my sister had also been pregnant before marriage. Since sex was something we never discussed, it made me very angry and embarrassed that my mother would mention it that way in front of George.

*The heaviness I had felt before
came back.*

When George started to put pressure on me sexually, the heaviness I had felt before I became a Christian came back. It was such a disappointment, since all the other men I'd known had also done that to me. But I felt that I really cared for George and I gave in to him, figuring, "That's just the way men are." A subtle change took place in my thinking at that time, the beginnings of a disillusionment with Christianity.

I was pregnant when we married, but a month later I lost my baby and spiralled down into depression. George began bringing marijuana home for us to smoke together, and I again contemplated suicide.

We were attending church sporadically and hearing glorious stories of others' victories. I agonized over why we were struggling so much. People said we should be different because we were new creatures in Christ, and that just made me feel more rejected, confused and hopeless.

I thought that having a baby would perhaps fill the void in my life. It seemed that no one needed me and that having a child who depended on me might make me feel better. When I found I was pregnant, I told George I wasn't going to use pot anymore. He got angry and we fought over almost everything until our arguments became violent and he would often stomp out of the house.

I would be angry to the point of rage.

I continued to be depressed most of the time, but I didn't realize my need for help until after my son was born. I would become angry with him to the point of rage. Two-and-a-half years later when my daughter was born, I began having nightmares of my son molesting or hurting her, and I found myself overreacting to the simplest things he did wrong. This bothered me and I talked with friends and my pastor about it (not Pastor Simms), but they simply passed it off, saying, "You're a good mom."

I felt that the pastor rejected me because he expected a Christian to be able to live a perfect life. He was unkind and accusing and we did not feel welcome at that church. I also did not feel accepted by George's dad and step-mother, so we had conflict there as well.

Then George lost his job. It was at the time our associate pastor was moving to work at a church in another part of the state, and he suggested that we make a change and move with him, which we did.

We were in the middle of nowhere.

A job opened up for George on a ranch that put us out in the middle of nowhere. We worked seven days a week and seldom went to church as a family. It was a difficult time, but George and I did get closer, having to depend on each other instead of everybody else.

We lived there for two-and-a-half years. All during that time I sensed hatred from my husband's boss. He kept asking, "When are you leaving?" Finally, when we did leave, he didn't come to the farewell dinner the staff arranged for us.

We were offered a part-time job and given money to move back to our previous town. This angered the pastor who had invited us to move with him, so he disassociated himself from us as well.

I continued to live in torment, hearing voices, having terrible nightmares and drinking. I was anorexic, had struggles with suicide and was masochistic, cutting myself as I had in grade school.

When I went to church, it was torment for me.

After the move, George and I began attending the church my brother and his wife were attending, and I really loved Pastor Simms. He seemed to genuinely care about people. Yet, when I went to church it was torment for me. Suddenly I would feel an intense hatred for him. As I looked at him, flashes of terrible things happening to him would fill my mind. I dreaded it and looked for excuses not to go.

A friend told me about a care group for victims which I attended for a long time, but it was hard. The minute I entered the care group, the voices in my head and the horrible thoughts got worse. Nevertheless, I was able to let some of my anger go and not vent my rage against my son all the time. That helped me because I had felt so guilty, like I was destroying my son.

He didn't make me feel like I was going crazy.

When I started counseling with Pastor Simms, I looked forward to every session. He was the first one who didn't just tell me that I was a new creature in Christ, that old things had passed away and I shouldn't be having any problems. Never did he make me feel like I was going crazy. I remember the first time I told him I was hearing voices in my head. He didn't laugh at me; he believed me.

Pastor Simms went through a lot trying to help me. I called him repeatedly, and when I struggled with suicide, he really supported me.

I was in a cycle of bulimia for two years, but I never

told my husband about it. I don't know why, because he already knew of my struggle with drinking, voices and suicidal thoughts. But when I was hospitalized for a month because of my eating disorder, it was a major shock to him, and he felt betrayed.

Later, George told me that just before I was released from the hospital, he had slept with a girl from work. That sent me into shock. I didn't want to deal with that or anything: not the voices that tormented me every time I went to church . . . not the things that happened before, during or after the hospital . . . not my childhood . . . not anything. For two months, I withdrew to my house and closed up inside myself.

> *I knew that somehow the Lord didn't want me to live like this.*

That's when Pastor Simms gave me the brochure about Dr. Anderson's seminar. I wanted to go because I knew that somehow the Lord didn't want me to live like this for the rest of my life.

Listening to Neil was like hearing the story of my life. He talked about people hearing voices and thinking of suicide, and that was me. His teaching gave me incredible hope, until the last day when we were asked to go through the prayers of the Steps to Freedom. On that day I got terribly sick to my stomach, my head felt like it was going to explode, and I thought I was going to throw up.

I moved to the back of the auditorium and finally left. I just couldn't stand it. After awhile, I forced myself to return; it was at the time when everyone was going through the forgiveness prayers. The voices inside me were screaming. I felt there was no one I was mad at, no one to forgive. Everyone was perfect; the only problem was me.

> *Just thinking about it would make me start crying.*

A couple of weeks later, I called Pastor Simms and told

him that I couldn't make the list of people to forgive in a group setting. Besides, when I was sitting in the back of the church there had been no one crying around me. No one else seemed to be struggling with anything, while just thinking about my problems brought me to tears. I didn't want to make a fool out of myself.

Pastor Simms said he had heard about another pastor who could take me through the prayers and that he would make an appointment and even go with me if I wanted. The day of the appointment, he met me there. I was feeling very nervous, but immediately felt safe as Pastor Simms and I sat down in Pastor Jones's office. I had never met this man before, yet as I looked into his face I sensed a peace and knew he was sincere and caring. He began by saying that if anything caused interference, such as the voices or feeling sick, I should let him know so that we could stop and pray, and it would go away.

I'd had daily, constant headaches since childhood, and they had increased in intensity during the last three years, ever since I went to the first care group. And now my head began to pound. When we came to the step on forgiveness, I got sick to my stomach as I had at the seminar. My hands were trembling. The voices were so loud they about drove me crazy, and I remember asking, "Don't you hear this?" At each one of these interferences, Pastor Jones prayed or led me to pray, "In the name of Jesus, I command you, Satan, to leave my presence," and the disturbance quieted. Going through those steps was the hardest thing I have ever done in my entire life, but with Pastor Jones's help, I did it.

I knew that things were now different.

At first, it didn't seem like anything had changed. But then my mom came over and criticized my housekeeping as she had so often in the past. When that happened and it didn't bother me, I knew things were different! I was apprehensive starting back to church, but that was different, too. I enjoyed the worship and listening to Pastor Simms, and for the first time I could hear what he was saying because there were no voices. I don't think I've ever smiled so much! I'm so grateful for Pastor Simms's unconditional love that kept pulling me back to the church.

I have underlined all of the verses about who I am in Christ in my Bible. I still have lying thoughts condemning and accusing me, but I don't hold on to them like I used to. I recognize them sooner. Life still has its problems, but it is the difference between night and day, nothing like it was before. Actually, my whole outlook has been totally different from the day I walked out of Pastor Jones's office.

*   *   *

Pat's husband, George, was so encouraged and glad that she had finally been released from so much torment that he was eager to find help for himself as well.

George's Story

Nothing in my life had worked to free me.

I was excited when I looked over the books Pat brought home from the seminar. *This will work,* I thought. And how I desperately needed the help it promised, because nothing else in my life had worked to free me from Satan's sexual stronghold that was destroying me and my marriage.

I grew up with a dad who was a perfectionist, the kind of dad with whom you do your best and it still isn't good enough. I'd hit the ball over the fence in the backyard and he would say, "Well, that was good, but let me show you a better way to swing the bat."

My parents divorced when I was about five, and even though I was very young my mother began to depend on me. Then she married again, and my stepdad was an alcoholic and verbally abusive. As I grew up I worked for him and he, too, would tell me how much he needed me. I believe it was because of that I developed the attitude of needing to work for acceptance and approval, something I tried very hard to do.

My dad had sexual-intercourse types of pornography.

The first time I saw pornography was when I was still with my real dad. He had some very vivid sexual-intercourse types of pornography. Also, my grandfather had a cabin with full centerfold pictures from *Playboy* on the walls. Both my dad and granddad had an attitude of disrespect and exploitation toward women.

My grandfather was also a 32nd degree Mason. He wore a Mason ring and was very politically influential in the city in which he lived. When he died, his funeral was a Mason funeral.

When I was thirteen, I began attending a Catholic school with a small student body. I wanted to be accepted, so I responded when one of the guys who seemed very popular showed an interest in me. He invited me over to his house when the only other person there was his older brother. We went into his bedroom and he wanted to have sex with me. I remember thinking, *I don't really want to do this, but I will if you will be my friend.* I had never had a desire for guys before, but somehow there seemed to be a seed planted at that time that had a profound impact on my behavior.

Pornography was my way of feeling good.

I never felt good about myself. I never felt accepted, so pornography was my way of feeling good. I never bought pornographic magazines myself because I could see all that I wanted from my dad's supply. I devoured my dad's *Playboy* magazines and fantasized about the women pictured there, as well as those in the women's sections of catalogs.

I began masturbating when I was fourteen. I would pick out a girl in high school and then I would go home at night and think about her and masturbate. I fantasized about the girls, but I didn't date any of them—I didn't talk with them and I didn't want a relationship. I just wanted sexual gratification. The whole focus was sexual.

I had intercourse for the first time when I was seventeen, and that wasn't even a date. I met the girl in a mall where we were introduced by a mutual friend, and then we went to her house and had sex together.

When I was eighteen, I began to date. One date was the girl next door. The thing I remember about her is that I couldn't stand her laugh, but that didn't keep me from having sex with her. Again, it was all a sexual focus; I didn't even want to know her. That became a concern to me, because I felt I might never be able to really love a girl but would just keep finding things wrong that would break the relationship.

I would purposefully date only those girls I thought I could have a relationship with sexually, not looking for girls who had character or were respectable. Sex was all that I wanted.

I didn't know what my purpose was in life.

When I was twenty, I became totally depressed and, for about a year, I didn't date anyone. The Lord began to work in my life as a result of a human ecology class at college. I found out that our world is falling apart and that started a deep depression. To counteract that, I was smoking pot and drinking. I didn't know what my purpose was in life. I wanted to be loved, but I went with the wrong people. I wanted a future, but it frustrated me that there wasn't one.

During that time I was given a Gideon New Testament by someone who was handing them out at the college. I began reading it and later, when I saw the movie *The Ten Commandments*, I began reading the Old Testament.

As I read the New Testament, it excited me that God could have a relationship with me. As I read the Old Testament, all I could think about was the rules I had broken. I thought, *How am I going to get out from under this? I'm so guilty.* So I got more depressed.

Another thing that made me feel helpless was my marijuana habit. I knew it was wrong. I wanted to quit but I couldn't. I remember telling God, "Please do something. I want to quit. I want to be right before You, but I just keep hurting You and sinning against You."

It dawned on me that God was talking to me.

One day I took my bicycle, lunch and Gideon New Testament and said, "I'm going to go out and have lunch with God." I read the parable of the sower and, as I did, I understood the meaning. When I read the interpretation in the following verses and saw that my understanding was correct, it dawned on me that God was actually talking to me through the Bible. But I couldn't understand why God would when I had broken all His laws.

I knew that I needed to break my unhealthy relationships, so I moved back to the state where my mother lived. That summer I met a lesbian who invited me to her home with some other guys. They invited me to a bar where I began drinking and ended up French-kissing a guy. A powerful, lustful feeling came over me, far more powerful than anything I had ever felt being with a girl, and it scared me to death. It was an inflamed, aggressive desire that came out of nowhere, and I realized that I was opening myself up to homosexuality. That scared me so much that I quit.

Around that time I read a weird book by Roy Masters who talked about Jesus in a twisted way. I got it at a bookstore in the mall where they were having a seminar on New Age. I started to meditate in my closet. I would put my hand in front of my head and bring it toward me and it was supposed to feel like my hand went right into my head. I was searching, and because this teaching had a "Jesus" flavor to it, I was open to it.

I probably would have gone further into New Age had someone not left a copy of *The Late Great Planet Earth* with my sister. I read the whole book and, when I finished, I went outside and asked Jesus to be my Savior. However, I wasn't sure that He really was.

> ### *That's when I gained the assurance of my salvation.*

A friend said, "You have to meet my grandmother. She can help you." When I did, I thought, *I've never met anyone so on fire for the Lord.* She had a deep personal relationship with Jesus. After talking with her one evening, I realized that I needed to take a definite stand and surrender my life to Christ. I went with her to church the next morning and when the invitation was given, she asked me if I wanted her to go forward with me. I told her, "You don't need to. I'm on my way," and that's when I gained my assurance of salvation.

From that day, I really wanted to obey the Lord. For a solid year I didn't masturbate and had no sexual problems of any kind. Then I moved back to the state where my dad lived and went to work at the Christian conference center where I met Pat.

I loved the Lord and just wanted to serve Him, but one day I was listening to a national Christian radio program and the speaker said something that gave the enemy a loophole. He talked about masturbation and didn't really treat it as a sin. He spoke of it lightly and said it was only a problem if it occurred over a long period of time. When I heard that, I went home that very night and said, "Well, if You understand, Lord, then I guess I can do that." The bondage was back, and once I started, it continued for years, even long into my married life.

A lot of girls worked at the conference center, but Pat stood out from them. I liked her quiet personality and I wanted to help her with her problems. She was also attractive and after a while we dated. Then I realized I loved her and wanted to marry her.

That marriage could have been so great, but I messed it up by coaxing her into having sexual intercourse with me before marriage. I'm responsible for that. She said later that she thought, *Why does he want to do this? We're going to get married.* But she didn't express herself and I wasn't sensitive to her feelings. I know the Lord has forgiven me, but this had its effect. The marriage night was a disappointment for her and for me.

Everything was out of control.

With my sexual addictions and Pat's harassment with voices, nightmares, anger and depression, you can imagine what our marriage was like: Everything was out of control.

While doing some extra work for my dad, I found explicit pornography in his desk and would look at that and masturbate. Then I found that he had videotapes. I had never seen a pornographic video before, and it was so powerful I couldn't believe it. It was ten times more powerful than a magazine. My sexual desire was building and building and got to the place where every time I looked at a girl it would be with lust.

At the same time Pat was trying to get free from her past through counseling with Pastor Simms, there was a girl at work to whom I became sexually attracted. It was like "The grass is greener on the other side." I was tempted on and off for about six months—a little cat and mouse thing, very subtle. The devil had set it all up, but I took the bait and had an affair with this girl. And the saddest part is that it happened at a time when Pat was in the hospital trying to get help. Afterward, I cried all night long, consumed with guilt like a huge rock on my heart. I was afraid I would lose my marriage. God had given Pat and me so much, and I took the chance of throwing it all away.

I was so totally bound. I had developed a strong desire for oral sex. One time, just before Pat went to the conference, I looked at myself in the bathroom mirror before taking a shower and felt like someone was grabbing me for sex. Another time I awoke at night feeling a woman on top of me with her mouth on me. It was a physical thing, beyond a dream. I know that there was something more than me involved, but there was no other person in the room.

*I had an immediate confidence
that I was free.*

After Pat went to the conference and I read the books she brought home, I wanted to go to see Pastor Jones, the one who led her through the Steps to Freedom. I was ready; I knew I needed that.

The appointment was arranged and I went. Afterward, I had an immediate confidence that I was free: The sexual desires were gone, but now my concern was whether I could stay free or if the bondage would return again.

I have to be honest in saying that even after I saw Pastor Jones and went through the Steps to Freedom, I did fall back into masturbation a few times. But I am learning how to resist now, and I know that when I fall it is an act of my will, a behavior pattern, not an uncontrollable compulsion. I know that I am loved, forgiven and accepted by God, and I want my mind to be renewed and transformed by Him.

I used to think the battle with Satan was already over and that we couldn't have that kind of problem. I thought we had a new nature and it was just the flesh we were struggling with, not a spiritual issue. Now I know that just as there are angels around, so there are spirits around, and that they can suggest things to you but you don't have to choose to do them.

Pat was the one who reminded me of this by saying, "You have a choice." When she said that, it all came back to me. Jesus said, "You shall know the truth and the truth shall make you free" (John 8:32). He is the truth and He has set me free. As I depend on Him, obey Him and choose His truth, He's keeping me free.

*   *   *

A Ministry for the Church

Pastor Jones (a former student) got involved in helping to free people from spiritual bondage when he sat through a counseling session that he asked me to lead. He has since taken further training and has set up a group called S.W.A.T. (Spiritual Warfare Against Trauma!) Not only has he personally helped many find freedom in Christ, but he has seen several from his congregation receive training to help others as well. I always encourage pastors not to attempt this ministry alone as they will quickly get swamped and, eventually, forsake other important ministries of the church.

If your church is going to take this vital ministry seriously, then start with a small group of the most spiritually mature people whom you can prayerfully select. These people must themselves be free in Christ and living a balanced life. They must be committed to the authority of Scripture and the study of God's Word.

Patience is a prerequisite since no session can be done in the short time that is normally allotted for Christian counseling. If you start to lead a person through the Steps to Freedom, finish them in that session. If you don't work through all of the steps to a resolution, that person will leave and have the worst week of his life. The only exception is when you are dealing with severely traumatized people, which we shall look at in the last chapter.

The Spiritual Side of Addiction

George's statement, "There was something more than me involved," brings up further issues on sexual addiction. I have already said that there is a spiritual side to addictive behaviors, but what he was experiencing is referred to as *incubi* and *succubi* (Latin terms for male and female sexual spirits). Most people will never divulge having had that kind of experience because it is so perverted. If I know that there has been incest or major sexual addiction, I ask counselees if they have ever felt like a presence was coming at them for the purpose of sex. Oftentimes the image they see will be a man with a goat bottom or a woman with a snake bottom or any variety of grotesque images. Sometimes they wake up compulsively masturbating.

One man felt something fondling his genitals at night and at first thought it was his wife. Rather than stand against it, he participated with it. The experience grew until he could feel the weight of a female body upon him. Then he started to feel the presence in his car as he drove to work. Finally, he started to think, *What am I doing? Am I going crazy?* Since he participated with it, it grew in intensity and wouldn't go away.

When he saw me, he was going to bed at night with a Bible between his legs and pictures of Jesus on his body in an effort to stop that attack. No, it didn't work! He was not freed from that until he renounced his involvement with the sexual spirit, renounced using his body as an instrument of un-righteousness, and then asked God to forgive him. This sexual bondage can be really sick and evil. I have had people tell me that they feel a compulsion to tie something around their neck while they masturbate, and some people have thus died of auto-erotic asphyxiation.

The Addictive Nature of Perversion

George's brief encounter with homosexual behavior vividly depicts the diabolical nature of perverted sex. The rush that he felt when kissing the man, like the rush from mind-altering drugs, was not from his natural self nor from God. Willfully going against God's standards opens the door for Satan's sirens, and feeling that high is intoxicating and enslaving. Never indulge in perverted sex in the first place, but if you have already done so, renounce it immediately and determine to flee from immorality. Paul summarizes this in Romans 13:12-14:

> The night is almost gone, and the day is at hand. Let us therefore lay aside the deeds of darkness and put on the armor of light. Let us behave properly as in the day, not in carousing and drunkenness, not in sexual promiscuity and sensuality, not in strife and jealously. But put on the Lord Jesus Christ, and make no provision for the flesh in regard to its lusts.

10

Ritual Abuse and MPD

While conducting a conference in another state, I was asked to visit a young woman hospitalized in a psychiatric unit. She had read my books and wanted to see me. Her doctor permitted it, but a nurse had to be present and the session had to be taped. Marie had been ritually abused as a young child. I knew I wasn't going to be able to resolve much in the hour I was allotted, so I just tried to offer her some hope. To accomplish anything significant, the initial session with ritual abuse victims may take several hours.

I asked for her cooperation by sharing with me any mental opposition that she might experience during our time together. As mentioned before, the mind is the control center. As long as Marie actively maintained control of her mind and brought to light the lying thoughts that were trying to distract her, we wouldn't lose control. It was a struggle, but Marie was able to maintain her focus for the hour. During that time I affirmed who she was as a child of God and the authority she had in Christ. I tried to help her understand the battle going on for her mind. As I started to leave, a different voice spoke out, "Who are you, why don't you like me?"

What was that? A demon? An alter-personality? Your theological education and biblical world view will greatly influence your response. Since secular psychology doesn't accept the reality of the spiritual world, there is only one possible diagnosis: multiple personality disorder (MPD). In contrast, some deliverance ministries see only demons in such situations. Which is correct? How can you know? Are there other possible explanations?

Before you are too quick to answer, let me share another story. After a church speaking engagement, several people swamped me with questions. One inquirer was an attractive lady in her early thirties. She was describing her childhood abuse when her eyes started to glaze over. I could see that she was being mentally distracted and I didn't want her to be embarrassed. So I asked her if she would wait until the others left and then I made an appointment to see her the following week.

Elaine was an extremely intelligent lady with an established career. However, in her inner-personal life she was barely hanging on, even though she was seeing a secular counselor and attending a twelve-step recovery group. While sharing her story, she suddenly proclaimed that one of her multiples didn't want to leave. I asked if she had been diagnosed as having a multiple personality disorder (MPD). She said she had; her counselor had informed her that she had twelve alternate personalities.

I asked permission to address only her. After we walked through the Steps to Freedom, there was no trace of the multiples. In her case, I believe the voices were clearly demonic. In other extreme cases, I believe there is a combination of a spiritual stronghold and a fragmented mind caused by severe trauma.

A Fragmented Mind

What is a fragmented mind? It is a divided mind, the result of choosing to mentally detach from immediate, surrounding circumstances. Everybody chooses to do this in a limited sense. I remember times when my children were young when I would choose to disassociate from my surroundings. They would be arguing rambunctiously in the other room, and I would tune them out. I was caught up in what I was doing (maybe studying or watching my favorite sports on TV), and I consciously (or subconsciously) chose not to deal with them because I didn't want to deal with something unpleasant, or I just didn't want to be distracted from what I was doing.

Mentally, I was "out in my garden" as my wife would say. "Earth to Neil" was her way of getting me to tune in to what was going on around me.

No, I'm not weird. We all do that on a regular basis. People who live by the railroad tracks or airports learn to ignore the noise. A friend can be in the house when a train goes by and say, "How can you stand this?" And the home-owner replies, "Stand what? Oh, the train! It bothered me for about three weeks and now I don't even notice it." We choose to think about that which is true, lovely, pure, etc. (Philippians 4:8). We can choose not to deal with something that is unpleasant, to disassociate, and to think upon something else. But this can be unhealthy if we are detaching from reality as a means of coping. It can also become a pattern of denial.

Multiply the unpleasantness of children fighting and passing trains by one thousand, and you will get a sense of what it is like for those who suffer from a dissociative disorder. It is a defense mechanism caused by severe trauma whereby the person dissociates in order to survive. Unfortunately, the atrocities they have been subjected to are recorded in their memory bank. Physically, their eyes continue to see, their ears continue to hear, and their bodies continue to feel, but the mind chooses to ignore all those haunting horrors and creates an imaginary, "safe" world in which to live.

Only One Birth Certificate

How are we going to resolve this dilemma? First, I don't prefer the term "MPD." It gives the impression that there are many people present in one body. There is only one birth certificate and there will be only one death certificate for these people . . . only one name will be written in the Lamb's Book of Life . . . and only one person will stand before God some day and give account for the choices made in this life.

Those who attempt to surface the various personalities and integrate them recognize that there is usually one dominant self, and they usually identify that part as the host personality. The MPD picture as seen by most mental health experts looks like this:

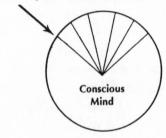

I don't believe this is the right perception. I prefer to think that there is only one person who has a fragmented mind. The picture would then look like this:

Fragmented portions of the mind hidden from memory

Conscious Mind

What to Do With the Old Self

The psychological integration of personalities goes beyond the scope of this book, but I do want to set forth the necessity of establishing these dear people in Christ and resolving their spiritual bondage first. In many cases, the victims themselves cannot tell if a voice in their minds is an alter personality or a demon. As I was taking one young lady through the Steps to Freedom, she suddenly confessed on the step dealing with rebellion, "I always thought that part of me was a personality." She renounced the evil spirit and her participation with it, and commanded it to leave. The change in her countenance was remarkable to both of us. Many godless counselors are trying to integrate demons into people's personalities, and many well-meaning pastors are trying to cast out personalities. Both extremes must be avoided.

Host personalities don't always like to admit that they are MPD and often resent the intrusion of other personalities that are less developed and sometimes embarrassing to them. Personalities are developed due to certain environmental factors. Each personality will involuntarily surface to perform the function for which it was developed. One personality may take over at work under pressure, and another personality may come out for social functions. Every MPD is different. In most cases fragmented personalities have not developed or learned to handle life in a Christ-centered way. In severe cases the fragmented personality may even be loyal to the cult that caused the fragmentation. Numerous cases have arisen where a committed Christian has split off at night and actually participated with satanists.

I usually explain to host personalities that their mind is like a house. They are the most dominant room in the house. As I help them clean up their room and establish them in Christ, they may be aware that there are other rooms in the house. The other rooms haven't been cleaned up, nor are they aware that they have been established in Christ. They must be acknowledged, won over, and set free from their past. Eventually they must all agree to come together in Christ. The following verses offer hope and provide direction for treatment.

> Now those who belong to Christ Jesus have *crucified the flesh* with its passions and desires. (Galatians 5:24)

> For you were formerly darkness, but *now you are light* in the Lord; walk as children of light. (Ephesians 5:8)

> Brethren, I do not regard myself as having laid hold of it yet; but one thing I do: *forgetting what lies behind* and reaching forward to what lies ahead, I press on toward the goal for the prize of the upward call of God in Christ Jesus. (Philippians 3:13, 14)

> Do not lie to one another, since you *laid aside the old*

self with its evil practices, and have put on the new
self who is being renewed to a true knowledge according to the image of the One who created him. (Colossians 3:9, 10)

When I was a child, I used to speak as a child, think
as a child, reason as a child; when I became a man, *I
did away* with childish things. (1 Corinthians 13:11)

Whole in Christ

Nowhere in Scripture are we told to resurrect the old self
or heal the flesh. We are made whole in Christ. "And we
proclaim Him, admonishing every man and teaching every
man with all wisdom, that we may present every man *complete in Christ*" (Colossians 1:28). We can't fix our pasts, but
we can be free from them.

I tell all fragmented children of God that in the deepest
part of their beings they are already whole. They are whole
because they are complete in Christ (Colossians 2:10). All we
need to do in our pastoral counseling process is resolve the
issues that caused them to fragment when they were young.
When those issues are resolved, they can be fully integrated.
I pray, asking the Lord to put them back together again and
make them complete in Him. Each individual personality must
decide to become a part of the whole person and complete
in Christ. We can't make them whole, but Jesus can. He came
to bind up the brokenhearted and restore the soul.

God redeemed us and established our identity in Christ
and then waits until we have an adequate support structure
before He peels off layers of the onion to show us more and
more of ourselves (see chapter two). I'm often asked, "What
if I have blocked out periods in my life that I can't remember?" Then keep pursuing God and be a good steward of
what God has entrusted to you. At the right time He "will
both bring to light the things hidden in the darkness and
disclose the motives of men's hearts; and then each man's
praise will come to him ..." (1 Corinthians 4:5). The only
reason it is necessary to surface the past is to recall the
experiences so that they can be resolved. If there isn't

anything hidden in the darkness, then don't worry about it. If there is, it will be revealed at the right time.

Deal With the Person

When past atrocities start to surface in a person, how can we tell if we are talking to a demon or a fragment of the mind? Sometimes it is difficult even if you have a lot of experience and spiritual discernment. Even the most experienced and mature people can be deceived. I certainly have been. In one sense, I don't try to differentiate; I always seek resolution by dealing only with the person. I never want the person to mentally lose control. Dialoguing with demons is always wrong, because that process totally bypasses the person and will surely lead to deception, since the demons all speak from their lying nature. People who believe what a demon tells them run the risk of being deceived.

At the time of the abuse, people may mentally disassociate as a defense mechanism in order to survive. When I counsel them, I don't want them to fall back into that old defensive pattern for survival. Christ is their defense now, and I do everything within my power to help them maintain control of their mind. If you encourage clients to repeatedly split off into fragmented personalities and explore their dissociative states without ever resolving anything or winning them over to Christ, you strengthen the existence of a defense mechanism instead of establishing Christ as their only necessary defense. Legitimate Christian counselors don't want to reinforce the existence of any other defense mechanism. Why this one? Let's expose it and find a better way to cope in Christ. If you use secular counseling techniques on multiples that don't even work for a whole person, the multiples will disassociate even more. We must learn to resolve issues in Christ so that they can get on with their lives.

Just like the person who is hearing voices, people with disassociative disorders will be reluctant to share what is really happening in their minds. They will function like adults in society, but take on different traits at home. They could behave like a parent in the living room and then behave like a child behind closed doors in the bedroom.

One counselor that I respect, who also understands the demonic, asks troubled clients, "Do you ever feel as though you aren't whole?" If they acknowledge that as the case, he asks permission to talk to the other part of them. The *only* reason it is ever necessary to do this is to get at the memory of what happened to cause the person to disassociate in the first place. I prefer asking the Holy Spirit to reveal the things "hidden in darkness."

If you do probe around in a person's altered states, I strongly recommend that you pray together first, and have the person pray, asking the Holy Spirit to guard her heart and mind and to protect them from any deception. In asking permission to address a fragment, make sure that the person remains actively involved. After you have found out what happened to cause the disassociation, resolve the issues by having the person forgive the offenders and renounce any cult or occultic experiences.

In every case, I strongly recommend that you go through the Steps to Freedom with the host personality first, before you start probing into his or her mind. The process of going through the steps will resolve the issues for the host personality and hopefully eliminate any demonic strongholds. I have had people switch personalities as they go through the steps. I usually just continue on if they are cooperative. Often there is a need for one personality to forgive another. One Christian group takes every personality through the steps. I don't believe that is necessary, but each part must resolve his or her own issues. I will probe only after going through the steps when I (or they) sense that there hasn't been complete resolution.

When the issues are resolved, I've never had to return to those same experiences with them again. The causes for fragmentation and demonic strongholds are simultaneously resolved. The person will continue to recall the experiences, but the past no longer has a hold on him. His mind begins to look like this:

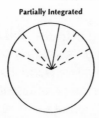

Partially Integrated

Fully Integrated

Complete in Christ

Old Things Have Passed Away

Many counselors who try to integrate personalities from the past into the host personality without resolving the issues have bizarre experiences with their clients. Some of them will take on the various personalities in destructive ways—some will wander into the night and then call home or get picked up by the police, unable to explain how they got there. This kind of behavior only happens when they disassociate. So why are we helping them to disassociate? Should we be encouraging victims to lose mental control by getting in touch with fragments of their minds without resolution? No person would want to leave a counseling session not knowing what happened. No one wants to disassociate. James 1:8 says that a double-minded man is "unstable in all his ways." It is that instability that we are trying to avoid by helping them to not lose mental control.

Whether the problem is a fragmented mind or a spiritual stronghold, I ask for one major cooperation from them. They must share with me what is going on inside. I explain that their minds are the control center, and if they don't lose control there, then we won't lose control in the session. There are two reasons why they may not share. First, they won't reveal what is going on in their minds if they suspect that you won't believe them. They may also be embarrassed by the foul nature of their thoughts. I tell them that it doesn't make any difference if those thoughts are coming from within or from a loud speaker on a wall, the only way they can be controlled by them is if they believe them. Sometimes I tell people that if they could see a demon, it would look like a little gnat with a great big mouth. Satan is a bully and a bluff. What we are up against is a major deception.

Some have a thought and immediately believe it or do it, not knowing that they have a "no" button. It's as though they have no will. Rather than believing the thought or acting upon it, I ask them to share what they are thinking with me. It is very intense working with severe cases because it is so easy to lose them. Sometimes I have them get up and walk around just to prove to themselves that they have control and can exercise it. Sometimes it may be necessary to back off by slowing the process down.

The second reason they may not share with you what is going on inside is because they are being intimidated. Usually it is a threat that they will be thrashed when they get home, or a threat of harm to others if they get free. Parents are often threatened that the evil spirits will attack their children. I sensed that one person wasn't sharing everything with me, so I asked her, "Are you being threatened that if you divulge what is going on you will be punished when you get home?" She acknowledged that she was. I said, "This has nothing to do with your house or when you get home, only your freedom now. If you resolve it here, it will also be resolved at home, because the problem isn't in your home, it's in your mind." She said immediately, "I wish you could prove that to me."

Getting it out in the open is what maintains control. God does everything in the light because He is the light of the world. The power of Satan is in the lie. When you expose the lie the power is broken. The power of the Christian is in the truth, so we are to speak the truth in love because we are members of one another.

A present popular psychological concept is the "inner child of the past." I have heard inner child of the past proponents say, "There are two people I am counseling, an adult and a little child within them." I disagree. Biblically, what is the inner-child of our pasts? Is it a part of our new identity in Christ, or is it a part of our old nature? Scripture assures us that we are not primarily products of our pasts but that we are new creations in Christ. "Therefore if any man is in Christ, he is a new creature; the *old things passed away;* behold, new things have come" (2 Corinthians 5:17).

Don't misunderstand me; I have seen people curl into fetal positions as they recall childhood experiences. I have seen spontaneous age regression in personality when horrible atrocities are recalled. I know that many have stopped developing emotionally because of traumatic experiences, but there is only one person sitting in front of me, not two. For his or her sake, I don't want that person to disassociate as she recalls a painful memory. I want her to learn a new way to deal with the past, a way based on truth.

"In reference to your former manner of life, you lay aside the old self, which is being corrupted in accordance with the lusts of deceit, and that you be renewed in the spirit of your mind, and put on the new self, which in the likeness of God has been created in righteousness and holiness of the truth" (Ephesians 4:22-24). We must acknowledge the emotional pain of our pasts and seek the healing that comes through forgiveness and establishing our new identity in Christ. We can't fix our pasts, but we can be free from them. In order to be free, we need to have a biblical means to get at repressed memories.

Getting at Things Passed Away

I'll say it again because it is so very important. We need to first establish a person's present identity in Christ before we attempt to expose the past. That is the order of Scripture for a very important reason. When we examine the past from our present position in Christ, we are assured that we already have victory in Him. We are already whole in the inner man and complete in Christ.

Suppose the most skilled secular counselor in the world was able to perfectly reconstruct a person's past, so that he or she is able to explain with precision what you are doing today and why you feel the way you do. So? Now what? The alcoholic would say, "You're right, that is precisely why I drink. Care to have a drink with me?" Reconstructing the past has value, but by itself it offers no resolution. There must be knowledge of who we are in Christ in order to adequately deal with past problems. We don't want to put a bandage on a symptom, we want to heal the disease which is separation from God.

Legitimate counselors know that they need to hear a person's story in order to resolve his or her conflict. Most counselor training programs focus on counseling techniques such as trust, warmth, congruence, accurate empathy, concreteness, immediacy, transparency, etc. These are essential if the person has total recall and just needs a trusting relationship in which to open up. But when memories are blocked, only God can reveal the things hidden in the darkness and disclose the motives of our hearts (1 Corinthians 4:1-5).

God Brings Things to Light

"It is He who reveals the profound and hidden things; He knows what is in the darkness, and the light dwells with Him" (Daniel 2:22). Satan does everything in the dark; like a thief in the night, he fears exposure. However, when a child has been subjected to satanic ritual abuse, even if it has been in his or her own home, be assured that God will bring it to light. "If they have called the head of the house Beelzebul, how much more the members of his household! Therefore do not fear them, for there is nothing covered that will not be revealed, and hidden that will not be known" (Matthew 10:25, 26).

> And this is the judgment, that the light is come into the world, and men loved the darkness rather than the light, for their deeds were evil. For everyone who does evil hates the light, and does not come to the light, lest his deeds should be exposed. But he who *practices the truth* comes to the light, that his deeds may be manifested as having been wrought in God.
> (John 3:19-21)

Most often, what God reveals will not be admitted to by the perpetrators. Most abusers will never admit their sin; satanists won't because they are under penalty of death should they ever reveal their deeds. Their deeds are evil and they hate the light, and rarely will they come to it.

I don't ask a person to try to remember what happened; I have him ask his Heavenly Father to reveal truth to him. "If you abide in My word, then you are truly disciples of Mine; and you shall know the truth, and the truth shall make you free" (John 8:31, 32). Facing the truth can be a frightening thing for many. Some would rather not face it, but freedom can come only as the truth is known—the total truth, the truth of God's word and the truth about ourselves. David cries out in Psalm 51:6, "Behold, Thou dost desire truth in the innermost being."

God's Spirit at Work

Making this truth known in the inner man is the great work of the Holy Spirit. Jesus said, "I will ask the Father, and He will give you another Helper, that He may be with you forever; that is the Spirit of truth" (John 14:16, 17). "But when He, the Spirit of truth, comes, He will guide you into all truth" (John 16:13). We don't have any power to reveal truth in the inner man, nor is there a learnable technique that can accomplish this task. Our part is to work with God as told in 2 Timothy 2:24-26:

> And the Lord's bondservant must not be quarrelsome, but be kind to all, able to teach, patient when wronged, with gentleness correcting those who are in opposition, if perhaps God may grant them repentance leading to the knowledge of the truth, and they may come to their senses and escape from the snare of the devil, having been held captive by him to do his will.

This passage is not a power model for deliverance, but a kind, patient, "able to teach" model that requires the pastor/counselor to be dependent upon God. Only God can grant repentance, leading to truth, which sets the captive free. Part of our role is to be patient; it takes time to process major atrocities. Satanic ritual abuse (SRA) victims require many sessions, and even then I am careful not to move too fast. If you move too fast, the person will lose control.

I haven't lost control in a long time, but if I did, I would stop the counseling process. Recently, and momentarily, I had a demon manifest and say, "Who the (blank) do you think you are?" "I'm a child of God," I said, "You shut up!" Immediately the lady was back. We can't be intimidated by these liars. I frequently have people say during a session that they have to get out of there. I say, "Okay, I'm not going to do anything to violate your mind." Every person who has left my office has been back within five minutes. Remember, it is the person's own responsibility to think.

Prayer Journaling

Memory retrieval as enabled by the Holy Spirit may be divided into four categories. The first is prayer journaling. I sometimes encourage people to personally ask God to reveal the truth to them at home, between appointments, and then to keep a journal of what the Holy Spirit brings to their minds. Some have a trusted prayer partner they ask to assist them. When we meet again, I help them process what they have remembered. It's not uncommon for them to bring two or three pages of sordid detail.

If they are trying to do this on their own, I ask them to pray for God's protection. I suggest that they record exactly what the Holy Spirit reveals, not questioning, only recording every minute detail. Many will wonder if they are making it all up. One lady visited the home she was raised in to see if the details about her neighborhood were what she thought the Holy Spirit enabled her to recall. To her surprise, the neighborhood was exactly what the Holy Spirit revealed, even though she hadn't seen the place for twenty-five years. My memory of early childhood is vague at best, so how can these people remember early childhood experiences with such clarity? They are not remembering it: God is revealing it to them.

Praying Through Stalemates

A second retrieval method is to have people in your presence, asking God to reveal what it is that is keeping them in bondage. Usually I will do this if our time together has come to a stalemate, or after I have gone through the Steps to Freedom and there has not been a complete resolution. We have processed all we could, but something has not yet surfaced.

One lady was working through forgiveness and stopped at her third-grade teacher. All she could remember was leaving the class and feeling bonded in some way to her. She forgave her for that, but we both knew that wasn't the real issue. I encouraged her to pray, asking the Lord to reveal what really happened in third grade. She did, and saw herself in a bathroom stall with the teacher, who was sexually abusing her.

How do we know that wasn't a mind game or satanic

deception? One way is to see if there is any external confirmation. In this case, classmates shared years later that her teacher treated her badly. Also, she was sent home bleeding from her uterus with the explanation that she fell, though she never did remember falling. The bonding was spiritual, due to the sexual abuse, not the psychological bonding that can take place because of a close teacher/student relationship.

Never put suggested thoughts into another person's mind, even if you suspect abuse, because the mind is very vulnerable to suggestions. The vague memory of an honest hug by a parent can be easily distorted into inappropriate fondling or worse. As a pastor/counselor, I pray for wisdom and guidance for myself, but I always have the person ask the Lord to reveal what it is that is keeping them in bondage. I would be suspicious of any details that come from a dream. Nightmares usually indicate some spiritual assault but are usually eliminated after a person has found her freedom in Christ. One lady accused her parents of sexual abuse because she had a dream, and a friend confirmed it through "words of knowledge." That is far too subjective to make accusations. There will almost always be some external confirmation of what they recall.

Satan attacks the minds of hurting people and does seek to discredit spiritual leaders by putting thoughts into the minds of their children or associates. I know of several cases where parents have been falsely accused by their children. Satan is crafty. If he can induce phony memories of ritual abuse and the accused are cleared of all charges, many will think that all the legitimate cases are phony as well.

What if people pray and nothing surfaces? Then I encourage them to continue their pursuit of God. Possibly the timing isn't right. Maybe there is nothing there and we need to explore another reason for their difficulties. You can only process that which you know. I don't think we ought to search for things in the past, but wait until God reveals the things hidden in the darkness.

Prayer for Light on Areas of Bondage

The third way is to ask the Lord to reveal specific areas

of bondage. Usually this is done as I walk people through the Steps to Freedom. In the first step, they pray and ask God to reveal all cult, occult, and non-Christian experiences they have had. After they pray, I ask them to check those involvements on a list of non-Christian experiences included in that step. But that list is not exhaustive; there are thousands of counterfeits, and sometimes people will add to the list. If I sense that they are brushing over that step, I will ask them to pray again that God will remind them of all the involvements they have had in this area. Chapter two of this book recounts the story of the woman who had completely forgotten that she had actively pursued the occult as a child. It was only after she had forgiven others that the Holy Spirit revealed her childhood pursuits.

When going through the forgiveness step, a person is asking God to reveal the names of people he needs to forgive. In most cases, some names will surface that he had consciously buried, and when he goes through the process of forgiving, God will often bring back memories that have consciously (or subconsciously) been buried in the past.

If there has been sexual abuse, I have the person ask the Lord to reveal every sexual offense so she can renounce each one, saying, "I renounce that (specific violation) of my body." When she is done, I lead her in a general declaration based on Romans 6:1, 2, 13 and 12:1, 2: "I renounce the use of my body as an instrument of unrighteousness, and I present my body to God as an instrument of righteousness, a living sacrifice Holy and acceptable unto God." If she is married, I will have her add, "I commit my body to my spouse only."

These people don't just remember an experience, they relive it. To wallow in the past is to keep them in bondage and strengthen the hold, so we should never reinforce what has happened by dwelling on it. When God grants repentance leading to the truth, we must participate with His leading, helping the person come to full repentance. Repentance literally means a "change of mind." The idea is, "I used to believe that; now I believe this." But the concept is much broader than mental acquiescence. Complete repentance means, "I used to walk one way, now I have totally turned around and I am walking according to the Way, the Truth, and the Life. I renounce the lie and all the satanic experiences that I have had, and I announce the truth and all the reality of salvation that is mine as a new creation in Christ."

Renouncing the Kingdom of Darkness

The fourth method of dealing with the past is to lead a person through several renunciations. I use this method early in the counseling process whenever a person has periods of his life blocked out. It is a generic means of checking out his past as well as resolving certain issues that accompany satanic ritual abuse (SRA). You have nothing to lose if there is no SRA.

In SRA, satanists do everything in direct opposition to Christianity. Satanism is the antithesis of Christianity. Satan is the anti-Christ. So I have clients renounce any possible involvement in the following way:

Kingdom of Darkness	Kingdom of Light
I renounce ever signing my name over to Satan or having my name signed over to Satan.	I announce that my name is now written in the Lamb's Book of Life.
I renounce any ceremony where I may have been wed to Satan.	I announce that I am the Bride of Christ.
I renounce any and all covenants that I made with Satan.	I announce that I am a partaker of the New Covenant with Christ.
I renounce all satanic assignments for my life, including duties, marriage, and children.	I announce and commit myself to know and do only the will of God and accept only His guidance.
I renounce all spirit guides assigned to me.	I announce and accept only the leading of the Holy Spirit.
I renounce ever giving of my blood in the service of Satan.	I trust only in the shed blood of my Lord Jesus Christ.
I renounce ever eating of flesh or drinking of blood for satanic worship.	By faith, I eat only the flesh and drink only the blood of Jesus in Holy Communion.
I renounce any and all guardians and satanist parents who were assigned to me.	I announce that God is my Father and the Holy Spirit is my Guardian by which I am sealed.
I renounce any baptism and all sacrifices that were made on my behalf by which Satan may claim ownership of me.	I announce that only the sacrifice of Christ has any hold on me. I belong to Him. I have been purchased by the blood of the Lamb.

For SRA victims, the above renunciations are an expansion of the confession made by the early church, "I renounce you, Satan, and all your works and all your ways." However, even the above renunciations are generic since all SRA victims have been subjected, in one form or another, to the above rituals and more. Again, as the Holy Spirit reveals the specific things hidden in darkness, they must be specifically renounced.

The Way Satan Counterfeits

Satanists refer to the book or scroll where they have people sign their names as the "goat's book of life," and often the signing is done in blood. A colleague at our seminary brought in a fifteen-year-old girl who had participated in satanism for ten years. It was difficult, but she gave her heart to the Lord. Without looking up, she said, "It's burning up, it's burning up." "What's burning up?" I asked. "The book I wrote my name in!" Apparently, God gave her a visual aid to help her accept the fact that her name is now written in the Lamb's Book of Life.

Satanists also perform wedding rituals where the child or adult is wed to Satan, and afterward the wedding is consummated in horrible sexual violations. Eating flesh and drinking blood are also a regular part of their rituals as a counterfeit of John 6:53, "Truly, truly, I say to you, unless you eat the flesh of the Son of Man and drink His blood, you have no life in yourselves." John equates eating and drinking with believing (John 6:40, 47, 48), but they take it literally. One person I counseled couldn't eat meat because it solicited the recall of eating raw flesh. He renounced it in light of 1 Timothy 4, where we are told that it is those who are deceived (verse 1), who "forbid marriage and advocate abstaining from foods, which God has created to be gratefully shared in by those who believe and know the truth. For everything created by God is good, and nothing is to be rejected, if it received with gratitude" (verses 3, 4).

Ritualistic cutting for the purpose of shedding blood is common in many pagan religions where people ritualistically cut themselves as a counterfeit of Christ shedding His blood for us. The idea is, we will become our own god and shed our own blood for ourselves. All blood pacts need to be renounced, even "innocent" ones that were made with "blood brothers" and "blood sisters."

Satanic Sacrifice

Sacrificing is an attempt to establish ownership. We were redeemed "with precious blood, as of a lamb unblemished and spotless, the blood of Christ" (1 Peter 1:19).

In satanic ritual abuse, children are often forced to do the sacrificial killing themselves for two reasons. First, it conditions them for future participation in the ritual. Often drugs are the means whereby they are forced into this compliance with horrible sexual abuse and sacrificial rituals. Or, they may comply because of threats of harm to others, as was the case with one girl who was told that her brother would be harmed if she didn't participate. And why do satanists perform these killings on innocent victims like babies, fetuses, and animals? They say, "Your God sacrificed His only Son, who was perfectly innocent." For them, the greater the sacrifice, the greater the power. And satanists are into power.

Second, children are forced to kill because it forces them into secrecy—a person is not about to tell the outside world that she killed an innocent child or animal. Her memories may be blocked out, but when she does recall the atrocities years later, she still can't share them because she assumes responsibility for having done it. She must take into account drugs or other ways she was forced into compliance. These people fear for their lives, both then and now, because they know that sacrificing a life means nothing to a satanist. If they refuse to do the killing during ritual, then they will be killed, or at least they fear that possibility. Fear is what keeps them from disclosing the things done in darkness, and the present guilt and grief they feel is overwhelming.

Symptoms of Ritual Abuse

Two major symptoms of SRA are sexual dysfunction and zero affect (no emotion). Most satanic rituals are ripping, banging, violent sexual orgies, not sex as normal humans would experience it. The ultimate high is sexual orgasm at the time of the kill. This is the stuff extremely hard-core pornography is made of, using animals, objects, and sadomasochistic acts. In fact, hard-core pornography and satanism are often linked together.

Those who have been abused in this way need to renounce this sexual use of their body and forgive the sexual abusers. One victim could clearly recall twenty-two sexual abusers. Could we honestly expect her to forgive those multiple offenses? Remember, for her to forgive them is not excusing what the abusers did; it is freeing her from the past.

The zero affect is the result of programming. The victims are conditioned to believe that if they cry, someone or something will be killed, or great physical harm will come upon them. One lady recalled her pregnancy being aborted for the purpose of sacrifice. When she screamed in horror, they told her that if she cried another baby would die. As a result, she had not been able to cry for years. I told her to renounce that experience and renounce the lie that her crying would result in the death of anything or anyone. As soon as she did, she sobbed for several minutes.

A pastor's wife drove several miles to attend a conference. She had just started recalling SRA and was puzzled by her own inability to cry. She had no specific memories of events, only vague, shadowy images. I said, "You may not understand this, but I want you to renounce the lie that your crying would result in the death of anyone." As soon as she did, a tear started to trickle down her cheek.

Every specific assignment needs to be renounced. Like curses, assignments are made during rituals. For instance, I was working through the step of forgiveness with one victim. When she came to her mother, she couldn't forgive her. Not because she didn't want to, but because she couldn't connect emotionally with one particular experience. She had already forgiven her father who took her to the rituals, which was a painful and emotional process that took a great deal of time. She could clearly recall one experience where her father raped her and she cried out to her mother to rescue her but she didn't. It was like she was telling a story but couldn't connect emotionally to the experience. (Usually when they describe the experience, there is a great deal of emotion expressed because they don't just recall it, they relive it.)

We weren't able to resolve that so we went on to the other names on her list (which I never prefer to do), and she came to the name of a woman she recalled from the SRA who, she said, "was assigned to be my mother."

"That's it," I exclaimed. "Renounce that assignment." She said, "I renounce the assignment of that woman being my mother and announce that I have only one mother who is (name)." As soon as she did that, she cried hysterically, "My mother abandoned me." She spent the next ten minutes reliving the horror of her mother rescuing her brother from her father, but not her.

Another person recalled a family being assigned to be her satanic parents and their son to be her husband. This was a prominent family in the church she was raised in. She, too, didn't have any emotional freedom to cry or feel deeply. She was impregnated by the son, and her baby was aborted and sacrificed. When she cried hysterically, a baby was put in her arms. That baby would also die if she cried, they said. When she renounced that lie, she was freed to feel emotion and cry. She also renounced the assignment of the son to be her husband. When she left my office, she said, "Now I can get married, now I can have children." Until those assignments are recalled and renounced, they keep people in bondage.

One lady recalled an assignment given to her when she was in the fourth grade. A young boy in the group was to be her husband and they were to bear a child. Any other man would reject her and any other offspring would be killed.

This lady eventually married another man, but was paranoid about being rejected by him and was fearful of having children. When I encouraged her to renounce that assignment, she became terrified. She told me she just couldn't do it, and I assured her that she not only could, she must. I learned later that her mind was being pummeled with lies and visions of babies dying. I said, "This has nothing to do with any future babies, this has only to do with your present freedom." I told her that God would protect any future offspring. She renounced the assignment, broke the satanic stronghold, and collapsed in tears. She is now free to have babies, understanding why she wasn't before.

As the Holy Spirit brings back memories, I have the person renounce the lies and assignments, proclaim the truth, and accept only God's will for his life. (Knowing God's will and understanding His leading is the subject of my book *Walking in the Light.*) This needs to be done specifically and verbally as memories are recalled.

It's Only the Lord Who Freed Captives

As we seek to help others, we find that every case is different and in each circumstance, we need to wait patiently upon the Lord and rely upon His leading, because He is the only One capable of setting captives free. Our role is to cooperate with God in helping His children find their identity and freedom in Christ.

You have heard from several dear people in this book who were desperately crying out to God for freedom. I pray that their stories will help you understand what is happening to many people in your church. Perhaps it is happening to you. It is my prayer that we have given you some hope and direction to find the freedom that Jesus purchased for you on the cross. God loves you. He wants you free *in* Christ!

Here is one final testimony, but this one you will recognize from Psalm 18:16-19 (NIV):

> He reached down from on high and took hold of me; he drew me out of deep waters. He rescued me from my powerful enemy, from my foes, who were too strong for me. They confronted me in the day of my disaster, but the LORD was my support. He brought me out into a spacious place; he rescued me because he delighted in me.

Praise His Name!

Appendix

Steps to Freedom in Christ

PREFACE

If you have received Christ as your personal Savior, He has set you free through His victory over sin and death on the cross. If you are not experiencing freedom, it may be because you have not stood firm in the faith or actively taken your place **in Christ.** It is the Christian's responsibility to do whatever is necessary to maintain a right relationship with God. Your eternal destiny is not at stake; you are secure in Christ. But your daily victory is at stake if you fail to claim and maintain your position in Christ.

You are not the helpless victim caught between two nearly equal but opposite heavenly super powers, Satan is a deceiver. Only God is omnipotent (all powerful), omnipresent (always present), and omniscient (all knowing). Sometimes the reality of sin and the presence of evil may seem more real than the presence of God, but that's part of Satan's deception. Satan is a defeated for, and we are in Christ. A true knowledge of God and our identity in Christ are the greatest determinants of our mental health. A false concept of God, a distorted understanding of who we are as children of God, and the misplaced deification of Satan (attributing God's attributes to Satan) are the greatest contributors to mental illness.

As you prepare to go through the *Steps to Freedom*, you

need to remember that the only power Satan has is the power of the lie. As soon as we expose the lie, the power is broken. The battle is for your mind. The control center is in your mind. If Satan can get you to believe a lie, he can control your life, but you don't have to let him. The opposing thoughts that you may experience can control you only if you believe them. If you are going through the steps by yourself, don't pay attention to any deception; i.e., lying, intimidating thoughts in your mind. Thoughts like, "This isn't going to work," "God doesn't love me," etc. can interfere only if you believe those lies. If you are going through the steps with a trusted pastor or counselor or lay encourager (which we strongly recommend if there has been severe trauma in your life), then share any thoughts you are having that are in opposition to what you are attempting to do. As soon as you expose the lie, the power of Satan is broke. *You must cooperate with the person trying to help you by sharing what is going on inside.*

Knowing the nature of the battle for our minds, we can pray authoritatively to stop any interference. The steps begin with a suggested prayer and declaration. If you are going through the steps by yourself, you will need to change some of the personal pronouns; i.e., "I" instead of "we."

STEPS TO FREEDOM IN CHRIST

Prayer

Dear Heavenly Father. We acknowledge Your presence in this room and in our lives. You are the only omniscient (all knowing), omnipotent (all powerful), and omnipresent (always present) God. We are dependent upon You for apart from Christ we can do nothing. We stand in the truth that all authority in heaven and on earth has been given to the resurrected Christ, and because we are in Christ, we share that authority in order to make disciples and set captives free. We ask You to fill us with Your Holy Spirit and lead us into all truth. We pray for Your complete

protection and ask for Your guidance. In Jesus' name. Amen.

Declaration

In the name and authority of the Lord Jesus Christ, we command Satan and all evil spirits to release (name) in order that (name) can be free to know and choose to do the will of God. As children of God seated with Christ in the heavenlies, we agree that every enemy of the Lord Jesus Christ be bound and gagged to silence. We say to Satan and all his evil workers that you cannot inflict any pain or in any way prevent God's will from being accomplished in (name's) life.

Preparation

Before going through the *Steps of Freedom*, review the events of your life to discern specific areas that might need to be addressed.

Family History

_____ Religious history of parents and grandparents
_____ Home life from childhood through high school
_____ History of physical or emotional illness in the family
_____ Adoption, foster care, guardians

Personal History

_____ Eating habits (bulimia, binging and purging, anorexia, compulsive eating)
_____ Addictions (drugs, alcohol)
_____ Prescription medications (What for?)
_____ Sleeping patterns and nightmares
_____ Raped or any sexual, physical, emotional molestation
_____ Thought life (obsessive, blasphemous, condemning, distracting thoughts, poor concentration, fantasy)
_____ Mental interference in church, prayer, or Bible study
_____ Emotional life (anger, anxiety, depression, bitterness, fears)
_____ Spiritual journey (Salvation: when, how, and assurance)

Now you are ready to begin. The following are seven specific steps to process in order to experience freedom from your past. You will address the areas where Satan most commonly takes advantage of us and where strongholds have been built. Christ purchased your victory when He shed His blood for you on the cross. Realizing your freedom will be the result of what you choose to believe, confess, forgive, renounce, and forsake. No one can do that for you. The battle for your mind can only be won as you *personally* choose truth.

As you go through these *Steps to Freedom*, remember that Satan will only be defeated if you confront him verbally. He cannot read your mind and is under no obligation to obey your thoughts. Only God has complete knowledge of your mind. As you process each step, it is important that you submit to God inwardly and resist the devil by reading aloud each prayer—verbally renouncing, forgiving, confessing, etc.

You are taking a fierce moral inventory and making a rock-solid commitment to truth. If your problems stem from a source other than those covered in these steps, you have nothing to lose by going through them. If you are sincere, the only thing that can happen is that you will get very right with God!

Step 1: Counterfeit vs. Real

The first step to freedom in Christ is to renounce your previous or current involvements with satanically-inspired occult practices and false religions. You need to renounce any activity and group which denies Jesus Christ, offers guidance through any source other than the absolute authority of the written Word of God, or requires secret initiations, ceremonies, or covenants.

In order to help you assess your spiritual experiences, begin this step by asking God to reveal false guidance and counterfeit religious experiences.

Dear Heavenly Father. I ask You to guard my heart and my mind and reveal to me any and all involvement I have had either knowingly or unknowingly with cultic or occult practices, false religions, and false teachers. In Jesus' name I pray. Amen.

Using the "Non-Christian Spiritual Experience Inventory" on this and the following page, carefully check anything in which you were involved. This list is not exhaustive, but it will guide you in identifying non-Christian experiences. Add any additional involvements you have had. Even if you "innocently" participated in something or observed it, you should write it on your list to renounce, just in case you unknowingly gave Satan a foothold.

Non-Christian Spiritual Experience Inventory
(Please check those that apply.)

OCCULT	CULT	OTHER RELIGIONS
Astral-projection	Christian Science	Zen Buddhism
Ouija board	Unity	Hare Krishna
Table lifting	Scientology	Bahaism
Dungeons and	The Way International	Rosicrucian
Dragons	Unification Church	Science of the Mind
Speaking in trance	Mormonism	Science of Creative Intelligence
Automatic writing	Church of the Living Word	Transcendental Meditation
Magic eight ball	Jehovah's Witness	Hinduism
Telepathy	Children of God	Yoga
Ghosts	Swedenborgianism	Echkankar
Seance	Herbert W. Armstrong	Roy Masters
Materialization	Unitarianism	Silva Mind Control
Clairvoyance	Masons	Father Divine
Spirit guides	New Age	Theosophical Society
Fortunetelling	Other _____	Islam
Tarot cards		Black Muslim
Palm reading		Other _____

Astrology
Rod and pendulum
   (dowsing)
Self-hypnosis
Mental suggestions or attempted to swap minds
Black and white magic
New Age medicine
Blood pacts or cut yourself in a destructive way
Fetishism (objects of worship)
Incubi and succubi (sexual spirits)
Other _____

1.   Have you ever been hypnotized, attended a New Age or parapsychology seminar, consulted a medium, spiritist, or channeler? Explain.

2.   Do you or have you ever had an imaginary friend or spirit guide offering you guidance or companionship? Explain.

3.   Have you ever heard voices in your mind or had repeating and nagging thoughts condemning you or that were foreign to what you believe or feel, like there was a dialog going on in your head? Explain.

4.   What other spiritual experiences have you had that would be considered out of the ordinary?

5.   Have you been involved in Satanic ritual of any form? Explain.

When you are confident that your list is complete, confess and renounce each involvement whether active or passive by praying aloud the following prayer, repeating it separately for each item on your list:

Lord, I confess that I have participated in_____. I ask your forgiveness, and I renounce_____.

If there has been any involvement in Satanic ritual or heavy occult activity (or you suspect it because of blocked memories, severe nightmares, sexual dysfunction, or bondage), you need to state aloud the special renunciations which follow. Read across the page renouncing the first item in the column on the Kingdom of Darkness and then affirming the first truth in the column on the Kingdom of Light. Continue down the page in that manner.

All Satanic rituals, covenants, and assignments must be specifically renounced as the Lord allows you to remember them. Some who have been subjected to Satanic Ritual

Abuse have developed multiple personalities in order to survive. Nevertheless, continue through the *Steps to Freedom* in order to resolve all that you consciously can. It is important that you resolve the demonic strongholds first. Eventually, every personality must be accessed, and each must resolve their issues and agree to come together in Christ. You may need someone who understands spiritual conflict to help you with this.

Special Renunciations for Satanic Ritual Involvement

Kingdom of Darkness	Kingdom of Light
I renounce ever signing my name over to Satan or having my name signed over to Satan.	I announce that my name is now written in the Lamb's Book of Life.
I renounce any ceremony where I may have been wed to Satan.	I announce that I am the Bride of Christ.
I renounce any and all covenants that I made with Satan.	I announce that I am a partaker of the New Covenant with Christ.
I renounce all Satanic assignments for my life, including duties, marriage, and children.	I announce and commit myself to know and do only the will of God and accept only His guidance.
I renounce all spirit guides assigned to me.	I announce and accept only the leading of the Holy Spirit.
I renounce ever giving of my blood in the service of Satan.	I trust only in the shed blood of my Lord Jesus Christ.
I renounce ever eating of flesh or drinking of blood for Satanic worship.	By faith I eat only the flesh and drink only the blood of Jesus in Holy Communion.
I renounce any and all guardians and Satanist parents who were assigned to me.	I announce that God is my Father and the Holy Spirit is my Guardian by which I am sealed.
I renounce any baptism in blood or urine whereby I am identified with Satan.	I announce that I have been baptized into Christ Jesus and my identity is now in Christ.
I renounce any sacrifices that were made on my behalf by which Satan may claim ownership of me.	I announce that only the sacrifice of Christ has any hold on me. I belong to Him. I have been purchased by the blood of the Lamb.

Step 2: Deception vs. Truth

Truth is the revelation of God's Word, but we need to acknowledge the truth in the inner self (Psalm 51:6). When David lived a lie, he suffered greatly. When he finally found freedom by acknowledging the truth, he wrote: "How blessed is the man . . . in whose spirit there is no deceit" (Psalm 32:2). We are to lay aside falsehood and speak the truth in love (Ephesians 4:15,25). A mentally healthy person is one who is in touch with reality and relatively free of anxiety. Both qualities should characterize the Christian who renounces deception and embraces the truth.

Begin this critical step by expressing aloud the following prayer. Don't let the enemy accuse you with thoughts such as: "This isn't going to work" or "I wish I could believe this but I can't" or any other lies in opposition to what you are proclaiming. Even if you have difficulty doing so, you need to pray the prayer and read the Doctrinal Affirmation.

Dear Heavenly Father. I know that You desire truth in the inner self and that facing this truth is the way of liberation (John 8:32). I acknowledge that I have been deceived by the father of lies (John 8:44) and that I have deceived myself (1 John 1:8). I pray in the name of the Lord Jesus Christ that You, Heavenly Father, will rebuke all deceiving spirits by virtue of the shed blood and resurrection of the Lord Jesus Christ. By faith I have received You into my life and I am now seated with Christ in the heavenlies (Ephesians 2:6). I acknowledge that I have the responsibility and authority to resist the devil, and when I do, he will flee from me. I now ask the Holy Spirit to guide me into all truth (John 16:13). I ask You to "Search me, O God, and know my heart; try me and know my anxious thoughts; and see if there be any hurtful way in me, and lead me in the everlasting way" (Psalm 139:23,24). In Jesus' name I pray. Amen.

You may want to pause at this point to consider some of

Satan's deceptive schemes. In addition to false teachers, false prophets, and deceiving spirits, you can deceive yourself. Now that you are alive in Christ and forgiven, you never have to live a lie or defend yourself. Christ is your defense. How have you deceived or attempted to defend yourself according to the following?

Self-deception

_____ Being hearers and not doers of the Word (James 1:22; 4:17)

_____ Saying we have no sin (1 John 1:8)

_____ Thinking we are something when we aren't (Galatians 6:3)

_____ Thinking we are wise in this age (1 Corinthians 3:18, 19)

_____ Thinking we will not reap what we sow (Galatians 6:7)

_____ Thinking the unrighteous will inherit the Kingdom (1 Corinthians 6:9)

_____ Thinking we can associate with bad company and not be corrupted (1 Corinthians 15:33)

Self-defense (defending ourselves instead of trusting Christ)

_____ Denial (conscious or subconscious)

_____ Fantasy (escape from the real world)

_____ Emotional insulation (withdraw to avoid rejection)

_____ Regression (reverting back to a less threatening time)

_____ Displacement (taking out frustrations on others)

_____ Projection (blaming others)

_____ Rationalization (defending self through verbal excursion)

For those things that have been true in your life, pray aloud:

Lord, I agree that I have been deceived in the area of

_____. Thank You for forgiving me. I commit myself to know and follow Your truth. Amen.

Choosing the truth may be difficult if you have been living a lie (been deceived) for many years. You may need to seek professional help to weed out the defense mechanisms you have depended upon to survive. The Christian needs only one defense—Jesus. Knowing that you are forgiven and accepted as God's child is what sets you free to face reality and declare your dependence on Him.

Faith is the biblical response to the truth, and believing the truth is a choice. When someone says, "I want to believe God, but I just can't," they are being deceived. Of course you can believe God. Faith is something you decide to do, not something you feel like doing. Believing the truth doesn't make it true. It's true; therefore we believe it. The New Age movement is distorting the truth by saying we create reality through what we believe. We can't create reality with our minds; we face reality. It's what or who you believe in that counts. Everybody believes in something, and everybody walks by faith according to what he or she believes. But if what you believe isn't true, then how you live (walk by faith) won't be right.

Historically the church has found great value in publicly declaring its beliefs. The Apostles' Creed and the Nicene Creed have been recited for centuries. Read aloud the following affirmation of faith, and do so again as often as necessary to renew your mind. Read it daily for several weeks.

Doctrinal Affirmation

I recognize that there is only one true and living God (Exodus 20:2,3) who exists as the Father, Son, and Holy Spirit and that He is worthy of all honor, praise, and glory as the Creator, Sustainer, and Beginning and End of all things (Revelations 4:11; 5:9,10; Isaiah 43:1,7,21).

I recognize Jesus Christ as the Messiah, the Word who

became flesh and dwelt among us (John 1:1,14). I believe that He came to destroy the works of Satan (1 John 3:8), that He disarmed the rulers and authorities and made a public display of them, having triumphed over them (Colossians 2:15).

I believe that God has proven His love for me because when I was still a sinner, Christ died for me (Romans 5:8). I believe that He delivered me from the domain of darkness and transferred me to His kingdom, and in Him I have redemption, the forgiveness of sins (Colossians 1:13,14).

I believe that I am now a child of God (1 John 3:1-3) and that I am seated with Christ in the heavenlies (Ephesians 2:6). I believe that I was saved by the grace of God through faith, that it was a gift and not the result of any works on my part (Ephesians 2:8).

I choose to be strong in the Lord and in the strength of His might (Ephesians 6:10). I put no confidence in the flesh (Philippians 3:3) for the weapons of warfare are not of the flesh (2 Corinthians 10:4). I put on the whole armor of God (Ephesians 6:10-20), and I resolve to stand firm in my faith and resist the evil one.

I believe that apart from Christ I can do nothing (John 15:5), so I declare myself dependent on Him. I choose to abide in Christ in order to bear much fruit and glorify the Lord (John 15:8). I announce to Satan that Jesus is my Lord (1 Corinthians 12:3), and I reject any counterfeit gifts or works of Satan in my life.

I believe that the truth will set me free (John 8:32) and that walking in the light is the only path of fellowship (1 John 1:7). Therefore, I stand against Satan's deception by taking every thought captive in obedience to Christ (2 Corinthians 10:5). I declare that the Bible is the only authoritative standard (2 Timothy 3:15,16). I choose to speak the truth in love (Ephesians 4:15).

I choose to present my body as an instrument of righteousness, a living and holy sacrifice, and I renew my mind by the living Word of God in order that I may prove that the will of God is good, acceptable, and perfect (Romans 6:13; 12:1,2). I put off the old self with its evil practices and put on the new self (Colossians 3:9,10), and I declare myself to be a new creature in Christ (2 Corinthians 5:17).

I ask my heavenly Father to fill me with His Holy Spirit (Ephesians 5:18), lead me into all truth (John 16:13), and empower my life that I may live above sin and not carry out the desires of the flesh (Galatians 5:16). I crucify the flesh (Galatians 5:24) and choose to walk by the Spirit.

I renounce all selfish goals and choose the ultimate goal of love (1 Timothy 1:5). I choose to obey the two greatest commandments, to love the Lord my God with all my heart, soul, and mind, and to love my neighbor as myself (Matthew 22:37-39).

I believe that Jesus has all authority in heaven and earth (Matthew 28:18) and that He is the head over all rule and authority (Colossians 2:10). I believe that Satan and his demons are subject to me in Christ since I am a member of Christ's body (Ephesians 1:19-23). Therefore, I obey the command to submit to God and to resist the devil (James 4:7), and I command Satan in the name of Christ to leave my presence.

Step 3: Bitterness vs. Forgiveness

We need to forgive others so that Satan cannot take advantage of us (2 Corinthians 2:10,11). We are to be merciful just as our heavenly Father is merciful (Luke 6:36). We are to forgive as we have been forgiven (Ephesians 4:31,32). Ask God to bring to mind the names of those people you need to forgive by expressing the following prayer aloud:

Dear Heavenly Father, I thank You for the riches of Your kindness, forbearance, and patience knowing that Your kindness has led me to repentance (Romans 2:4). I confess that I have not extended that same patience and kindness toward others who have offended me, but instead I have harbored bitterness and resentment. I pray that during this time of self-examination You would bring to my mind those people that I have not forgiven in order that I may do so (Matthew 18:35). I ask this in the precious name of Jesus. Amen.

As names come to mind, make a list of only the names.

At the end of your list, write "myself." Forgiving yourself is accepting God's cleansing and forgiveness. Also, write "thoughts against God." Thoughts raised up against the knowledge of God will usually result in angry feelings toward Him. Technically we don't *forgive* God, because He cannot commit any sin of commission or omission. But you need to specifically renounce false expectations and thoughts about God and agree to release any anger you have toward Him.

Before you pray to forgive those people, stop and consider what forgiveness is and what it is not, what decision you will be making, and what the consequences will be.

In the following explanation, the main points are in bold print:

Forgiveness is not forgetting. People who try to forget find they cannot. God says He will remember our sins "no more" (Hebrews 10:17), but God being omniscient cannot forget. Remember our sins "no more" means that God will never use the past against us (Psalm 103:12). Forgetting may be the result of forgiveness, but it is never the means of forgiveness. When we bring up the past against others, we are saying we haven't forgiven them.

Forgiveness is a choice, a crisis of the will. Since God requires us to forgive, it is something we can do. But forgiveness is difficult for us because it pulls against our concept of justice. We want revenge for offenses suffered. But we are told never to take our own revenge (Romans 12:19). You say, "Why should I let them off the hook?" That is precisely the problem. You are still hooked to them, still bound by your past. **You will let them off your hook, but they are never off God's.** He will deal with them fairly, something we cannot do.

You say, "You don't understand how much this person hurt me!" But don't you see, they are still hurting you! How do you stop the pain? **You don't forgive someone for their sake; you do it for your sake, so you can be free. Your need to forgive isn't an issue between you and the offender; it's between you and God.**

Forgiveness is agreeing to live with the consequences of another person's sin. Forgiveness is costly. You pay the price of the evil you forgive. You're going to live with those consequences whether you want to or not; your only choice is whether you will do so in the bitterness of unforgiveness or the freedom of forgiveness. Jesus took the consequences of your sin upon Himself. All true forgiveness is substitutionary, because no one really forgives without bearing the consequences of the other person's sin. God the Father "made Him who knew no sin to be sin on our behalf, that we might become the righteousness of God in Him" (2 Corinthians 5:21). Where is the justice? It's the cross that makes forgiveness legally and morally right: "For the death that He died, He died to sin, once for all" (Romans 6:10).

How do you forgive from your heart? You acknowledge the hurt and the hate. If your forgiveness doesn't visit the emotional core of your life, it will be incomplete. Many feel the pain of interpersonal offenses, but they won't or don't know how to acknowledge it. Let God bring the pain to the surface so He can deal with it. This is where the healing takes place.

Decide that you will bear the burden of their offenses

by not using that information against them in the future.
This doesn't mean that you must tolerate sin; you must always
take a stand against sin.

**Don't wait to forgive until you feel like forgiving; you
will never get there.** Feelings take time to heal after the
choice to forgive is made and Satan has lost his place
(Ephesians 4:26,27). **Freedom is what will be gained, not a
feeling.**

As you pray, God may bring to mind offending people
and experiences you have totally forgotten. Let Him do it
even if it is painful. Remember you are doing this for your
sake. God wants you to be free. Don't rationalize or explain
the offender's behavior. Forgiveness is dealing with your pain
and leaving the other person to God. Positive feelings will
follow in time; freeing yourself from the past is the critical issue
right now.

Don't say, "Lord, please help me to forgive," because He
is already helping you. Don't say, "Lord, I want to forgive,"
because you are bypassing the hard-core choice to forgive
which is your responsibility. Stay with each individual until
you are sure you have dealt with all the remembered pain—
what they did, how they hurt you, how they made you feel
(rejected, unloved, unworthy, dirty, etc.).

You are now ready to forgive the people on your list so
that you can be free in Christ, with those people no longer
having any control over you. For each person on your list,
pray aloud:

Lord, I forgive (name) **for** (specifically identify all offenses
and painful memories or feelings).

Step 4: Rebellion vs. Submission

We live in a rebellious generation. Many believe it is their
right to sit in judgment of those in authority over them.
Rebelling against God and His authority gives Satan an opportunity to attack. As our commanding general, the Lord says,

"Get into ranks and follow Me. I will not lead you into temptation, but I will deliver you from evil" (Matthew 6:13).

We have two biblical responsibilities in regard to authority figures: Pray for them and submit to them. The only time God permits us to disobey earthly leaders is when they require us to do something morally wrong before God or attempt to rule outside the realm of their authority. Pray the following prayer:

> **Dear Heavenly Father. You have said that rebellion is as the sin of witchcraft and insubordination is as iniquity and idolatry (1 Samuel 15:23). I know that in action and attitude I have sinned against You with a rebellious heart. I ask Your forgiveness for my rebellion and pray that by the shed blood of the Lord Jesus Christ all ground gained by evil spirits because of my rebelliousness would be cancelled. I pray that You will shed light on all my ways that I may know the full extent of my rebelliousness. I now choose to adopt a submissive spirit and a servant's heart. Amen.**

Being under authority is an act of faith. You are trusting God to work through His established lines of authority. There are times when employers, parents, and husbands are violating the laws of civil government which is ordained by God to protect innocent people against abuse. In those cases, you need to appeal to the state for your protection. In many states the law requires such abuse to be reported.

In difficult cases such as continuing abuse at home, further counseling help may be needed. And, in some cases, when earthly authorities have abused their position and are requiring disobedience to God or a compromise in your commitment to Him, you need to obey God not man.

We are all admonished to submit to one another as equals in Christ (Ephesians 5:21). However, there are specific lines of authority in Scripture for the purpose of accomplishing common goals.

Civil Government (Romans 13:1-7; 1 Timothy 2:1-4; 1 Peter
2:13-17)
Parents (Ephesians 6:1-3)
Husband (1 Peter 3:1-4)
Employer (1 Peter 2:18-23)
Church Leaders (Hebrews 13:17)
God (Daniel 9:5,9)

Examine each area and ask God to forgive you for those
times you have not been submissive, and pray:

**Lord, I agree I have been rebellious towards _____.
Please forgive me for this rebellion. I choose to be
submissive and obedient to your Word. In Jesus' name.
Amen.**

Step 5: Pride vs. Humility

Pride is a killer. Pride says, "I can do it! I can get myself
out of this mess without God or anyone else's help." Oh no
we can't! We absolutely need God, and we desperately need
each other. Paul wrote: "We worship in the Spirit of God and
glory in Christ Jesus and put no confidence in the flesh"
(Philippians 3:3). Humility is confidence properly placed. We
are to be "Strong in the Lord and in the strength of His might"
(Ephesians 6:10). James 4:6-10 and 1 Peter 5:1-10 reveal that
spiritual conflict follows pride. Use the following prayer to
express your commitment to live humbly before God:

**Dear Heavenly Father. You have said that pride goes
before destruction and an arrogant spirit before stum-
bling (Proverbs 16:18). I confess that I have lived
independently and have not denied myself, picked up
my cross daily, and followed You (Matthew 16:24). In
so doing, I have given ground to the enemy in my life.
I have believed that I could be successful and live
victoriously by my own strength and resources. I now
confess that I have sinned against You by placing my**

will before Yours and by centering my life around self instead of You. I now renounce the self-life and by so doing cancel all the ground that has been gained in my members by the enemies of the Lord Jesus Christ. I pray that You will guide me so that I will do nothing from selfishness or empty conceit, but with humility of mind I will regard others as more important than myself (Philippians 2:3). Enable me through love to serve others and in honor prefer others (Romans 12:10). I ask this in the name of Christ Jesus my Lord. Amen.

Having made that commitment, now allow God to show you any specific areas of your life where you have been prideful, such as:

_____ Stronger desire to do my will than God's will

_____ More dependent upon my strengths and resources than God's

_____ Sometimes believe that my ideas and opinions are better than others

_____ More concerned about controlling others than developing self-control

_____ Sometimes consider myself more important than others

_____ Tendency to think that I have no needs

_____ Find it difficult to admit that I was wrong

_____ Tendency to be more of a people pleaser than a God pleaser

_____ Overly concerned about getting the credit I deserve

_____ Driven to obtain the recognition that comes from degrees, titles, positions

_____ Often think I am more humble than others

_____ Other ways that you may have thought more highly of yourself than you should

For each of these that has been true in your life, pray aloud:

Lord, I agree I have been prideful in the area of _____.
Please forgive me for this pridefulness. I choose to
humble myself and place all my confidence in You.
Amen.

Step 6: Bondage vs. Freedom

The next step to freedom deals with habitual sin. People
who have been caught in the trap of sin-confess-sin-confess
may need to follow the instructions of James 5:16, "Confess
your sins to one another, and pray for one another, so that
you may be healed. The effective prayer of a righteous man
can accomplish much." Seek out a righteous person who will
hold you up in prayer and to whom you can be accountable.
Others may only need the assurance of 1 John 1:9: "If we
confess our sins, He is faithful and righteous to forgive us our
sins and to cleanse us from all unrighteousness." Confession
is not saying "I'm sorry," it's saying "I did it." Whether you
need the help of others or just the accountability of God, pray
the following prayer:

**Dear Heavenly Father. You have told us to put on the
Lord Jesus Christ and make no provision for the flesh
in regard to its lust (Romans 13:14). I acknowledge that
I have given in to fleshly lusts which wage war against
my soul (1 Peter 2:11). I thank You that in Christ my
sins are forgiven, but I have transgressed Your holy law
and given the enemy an opportunity to wage war in my
members (Romans 6:12,13; James 4:1; 1 Peter 5:8). I
come before Your presence to acknowledge these sins
and to seek Your cleansing (1 John 1:9) that I may be
freed from the bondage of sin. I now ask You to reveal
to my mind the ways that I have transgressed Your
moral law and grieved the Holy Spirit. In Jesus' precious name I pray. Amen.**

The deeds of the flesh are numerous. You may want to
open your Bible to Galatians 5:19-21 and pray through the

verses, asking the Lord to reveal the ways you have specifically sinned.

It is our responsibility to not allow sin to reign in our mortal bodies by not using our body as an instrument of unrighteousness (Romans 6:12,13). If you are struggling with habitual sexual sins (pornography, masturbation, sexual promiscuity) or experiencing sexual difficulty and intimacy in your marriage, pray as follows:

Lord, I ask You to reveal to my mind every sexual use of my body as an instrument of unrighteousness. In Jesus' precious name I pray. Amen.

As the Lord brings to your mind every sexual use of your body, whether it was done to you (rape, incest, or any sexual molestation) or willingly by you, renounce every occasion:

Lord, I renounce (name the specific use of your body) **with** (name the person) **and ask You to break that bond.**

Now commit your body to the Lord by praying:

Lord, I renounce all these uses of my body as an instrument of unrighteousness and by so doing ask You to break all bondage Satan has brought into my life through that involvement. I confess my participation. I now present my body to You as a living sacrifice, holy and acceptable unto You, and I reserve the sexual use of my body only for marriage. I renounce the lie of Satan that my body is not clean, that it is dirty or in any way unacceptable as a result of my past sexual experiences. Lord, I thank you that You have totally cleansed and forgiven me, that You love and accept me unconditionally. Therefore, I can accept myself. And I choose to do so, to accept myself and my body as cleansed. In Jesus' name. Amen.

Special Prayers for Specific Needs

Homosexuality

Lord, I renounce the lie that You have created me or anyone else to be homosexual, and I affirm that You clearly forbid homosexual behavior. I accept myself as a child of God and declare that You created me a man (or woman). I renounce any bondages of Satan that have perverted my relationships with others. I announce that I am free to relate to the opposite sex in the way that You intended. In Jesus' name. Amen.

Abortion

Lord, I confess that I did not assume stewardship of the life you entrusted to me, and I ask your forgiveness. I choose to accept your forgiveness by forgiving myself, and I now commit that child to You for Your care in eternity. In Jesus' name. Amen.

Suicidal Tendencies

I renounce the lie that I can find peace and freedom by taking my own life. Satan is a thief, and he comes to steal, kill, and destroy. I choose life in Christ who said He came to give me life and to give it abundantly.

Eating Disorders or Cutting on Yourself

I renounce the lie that my worthiness is dependent upon my appearance or performance. I renounce cutting myself, purging, or defecating as a means of cleansing myself of evil, and I announce that only the blood of the Lord Jesus Christ can cleanse me from my sin. I accept the reality that there may be sin present in me because of the lies I have believed and the wrongful use of my body, but I renounce the lie that I am evil or that any part of my body is evil. I announce the truth that I am totally accepted by Christ just as I am.

Substance Abuse

Lord, I confess that I have misused substances (alcohol, tobacco, food, prescription or street drugs) for the purpose of pleasure, to escape reality, or to cope with difficult situations, resulting in the abuse of my body, the harmful programming of my mind, and the quenching of the Holy Spirit. I ask Your forgiveness, and I renounce any Satanic connection or influence in my life through my misuse of chemicals or food. I cast my anxiety onto Christ who loves me, and I commit myself to no longer yield to substance abuse but to the Holy Spirit. I ask You, Heavenly Father, to fill me with Your Holy Spirit. In Jesus' name. Amen.

After you have confessed all known sin, pray:

I now confess these sins to You and claim through the blood of the Lord Jesus Christ my forgiveness and cleansing. I cancel all ground that evil spirits have gained through my willful involvement in sin. I ask this in the wonderful name of my Lord and Savior Jesus Christ. Amen.

Step 7: Acquiescence vs. Renunciation

Acquiescence is passively giving in or agreeing without consent. The last step to freedom is to renounce the sins of your ancestors and any curses which may have been placed on you. In giving the Ten Commandments God said: "You shall not make for yourself an idol, or any likeness of what is in heaven above or on the earth beneath or in the water under the earth. You shall not worship them or serve them; for I, the Lord your God, am a jealous God, visiting the iniquity of the fathers on the children, on the third and fourth generations of those who hate Me" (Exodus 20:4,5).

Familiar spirits can be passed on from one generation to the next if not renounced and your new spiritual heritage in Christ is not proclaimed. You are not guilty for the sin of any ancestor, but because of their sin, Satan has gained access to your family. This is not to deny that many problems are transmitted genetically or acquired from an immoral atmosphere. All three conditions can predispose an individual to a particular sin. In addition, deceived people may try to curse you, or Satanic groups may try to target you. You have all the authority and protection you need in Christ to stand against such curses and assignments. In order to walk free from past influences, read the following declaration and prayer to yourself first so that you know exactly what you are declaring and asking. Then claim your position and protection in Christ by making the declaration verbally and humbling yourself before God in prayer.

Declaration

I here and now reject and disown all the sins of my ancestors. As one who has been delivered from the power of darkness and translated into the kingdom of God's dear Son, I cancel out all demonic working that has been passed on to me from my ancestors. As one who has been crucified and raised with Jesus Christ and who sits with Him in heavenly places, I renounce all Satanic assignments that are directed toward me and my ministry, and I cancel every curse that Satan and his workers have put on me. I announce to Satan and all his forces that Christ became a curse for me (Galatians 3:13) when He died for my sins on the cross. I reject any and every way in which Satan may claim ownership of me. I belong to the Lord Jesus Christ who purchased me with His own blood. I reject all other blood sacrifices whereby Satan may claim ownership of me. I declare myself to be eternally and completely signed over and committed to the Lord Jesus Christ. By the authority that I have in Jesus Christ, I now command every familiar spirit and every enemy of the Lord Jesus Christ that is in or around me to leave my presence. I commit myself to my Heavenly Father to do His will from this day forward.

Prayer

Dear Heavenly Father. I come to You as Your child purchased by the blood of the Lord Jesus Christ. You are the Lord of the universe and the Lord of my life. I submit my body to You as an instrument of righteousness, a living sacrifice, that I may glorify You in my body. I now ask You to fill me with Your Holy Spirit. I commit myself to the renewing of my mind in order to prove that Your will is good, perfect, and acceptable for me. All this I do in the name and authority of the Lord Jesus Christ. Amen.

Once you have secured your freedom by going through these seven steps, you may find demonic influences attempting reentry days or even months later. One person shared that she heard a spirit say to her mind, "I'm back," two days after she had been set free. "No you're not!" she proclaimed aloud. The attack ceased immediately. One victory does not constitute winning the war. Freedom must be maintained. After completing these steps, one jubilant lady asked, "Will I always be like this?" I told her that she would stay free as long as she remained in right relationship with God. "Even if you slip and fall," I encouraged, "you know how to get right with God again."

One victim of incredible atrocities shared this illustration: "It's like being forced to play a game with an ugly stranger in my own home. I kept losing and wanted to quit, but the ugly stranger wouldn't let me. Finally I called the police (a higher authority), and they came and escorted the stranger out. He knocked on the door trying to regain entry, but this time I recognized his voice and didn't let him in." What a beautiful illustration of gaining freedom in Christ. We call upon Jesus, the ultimate authority, and He escorts the enemy out of our lives. Know the truth, stand firm, and resist the evil one. Seek out good Christian fellowship, and commit yourself to regular times of Bible study and prayer. God loves you and will never leave or forsake you.

After Care

Freedom must be maintained. You have won a very important battle in an ongoing war. Freedom is yours as long as you keep choosing truth and standing firm in the strength of the Lord. If new memories should surface or if you become aware of "lies" that you have believed or other non-Christian experiences you have had, renounce them and choose the truth. Some have found it helpful to go through the steps again. As you do, read the instructions carefully.

You should read *Victory Over the Darkness, The Bondage Breaker, Released from Bondage,* and *Living Free in Christ.* If you are a parent, read *The Seduction of Our Children. Walking Through the Darkness* was written to help people understand God's guidance and discern counterfeit guidance. Also, to maintain your freedom, we suggest the following:

1. Seek legitimate Christian fellowship where you can walk in the light and speak the truth in love.
2. Study your Bible daily. Memorize key verses. You may want to express the Doctrinal Affirmation daily and look up the verses.
3. Take every thought captive to the obedience to Christ. Assume responsibility for your thought life, reject the lie, choose the truth, and stand firm in your position in Christ.
4. Don't drift away! It is very easy to get lazy in your thoughts and revert back to old habit patterns of thinking. Share your struggles openly with a trusted friend. You need at least one friend who will stand with you.
5. Don't expect another person to fight your battle for you. Others can help but they can't think, pray, read the Bible, or choose the truth for you.
6. Commit yourself to daily prayer. You can pray these suggested prayers often and with confidence:

Daily Prayer

Dear Heavenly Father. I honor You as my sovereign Lord. I acknowledge that You are always present with me. You are the only all powerful and only wise God. You are kind and loving in all Your ways. I love You and I thank You that I am united with Christ and spiritually alive in Him. I choose not to love the world, and I crucify the flesh and all its passions.

I thank You for the life that I now have in Christ, and I ask You to fill me with Your Holy Spirit that I may live my life free from sin. I declare my dependence upon You, and I take my stand against Satan and all his lying ways. I choose to believe the truth, and I refuse to be discouraged. You are the God of all hope, and I am confident that You will meet my needs as I seek to live according to Your Word. I express with confidence that I can live a responsible life through Christ who strengths me.

I now take my stand against Satan and command him and all his evil spirits to depart from me. I put on the whole armor of God. I submit my body as a living sacrifice and renew my mind by the living Word of God in order that I may prove that the will of God is good, acceptable, and perfect. I ask these things in the precious name of my Lord and Savior Jesus Christ. Amen.

Bedtime Prayer

Thank You, Lord, that You have brought me into Your family and have blessed me with every spiritual blessing in the heavenly realms in Christ. Thank You for providing this time of renewal through sleep. I accept it as part of Your perfect plan for Your children, and I trust You to guard my mind and my body during my sleep.

As I have meditated on You and Your truth during this day, I choose to let these thoughts continue in my mind while I am asleep. I commit myself to You for Your protection from every attempt of Satan or his emissaries to attack me during sleep. I commit myself to You as my rock, my fortress, and my resting place. I pray in the strong name of the Lord Jesus Christ. Amen.

Cleansing Home/Apartment

After removing all articles of false worship from home/apartment, pray aloud in every room if necessary.

Heavenly Father. We acknowledge that You are Lord of heaven and earth. In Your sovereign power and love, You have given us all things richly to enjoy. Thank You for this place to live. We claim this home for our family as a place of spiritual safety and protection from all the attacks of the enemy. As children of God seated with Christ in the heavenly realm, we command every evil spirit, claiming ground in the structures and furnishings of this place based on the activities of previous occupants, to leave and never to return. We renounce all curses and spells utilized against this place. We ask You, Heavenly Father, to post guardian angels around this home (apartment, condo, room, etc.) to guard it from attempts of the enemy to enter and disturb Your purposes for us. We thank You, Lord, for doing this, and pray in the name of the Lord Jesus Christ. Amen.

Living in a Non-Christian Environment

After removing all articles of false worship from your room, pray aloud in the space allotted to you.

Thank You, Heavenly Father, for a place to live and to be renewed by sleep. I ask You to set aside my room (or portion of a room) as a place of spiritual safety for me. I renounce any allegiance given to false gods or spirits by other occupants, and I renounce any claim to this room (space) by Satan based on activities of past occupants or myself. On the basis of my position as a child of God and a joint-heir with Christ who has all the authority in heaven and on earth, I command all evil spirits to leave this place and never to return. I ask You, Heavenly Father, to appoint guardian angels to protect me while I live here. I pray this in the name of the Lord Jesus Christ. Amen.

Continue to seek your identity and sense of worth in Christ. Read the book *Living Free in Christ.* Renew your mind with the truth that your acceptance, security, and significance is in Christ by saturating your mind with the following truths. Read the entire list aloud morning and evening over the next several weeks.

IN CHRIST

I AM ACCEPTED:

John 1:12	I am God's child.
John 15:15	I am Christ's friend.
Romans 5:1	I have been justified.
1 Corinthians 6:17	I am united with the Lord, and I am one spirit with Him.
1 Corinthians 6:19,20	I have been bought with a price. I belong to God.
1 Corinthians 12:27	I am a member of Christ's body.
Ephesians 1:1	I am a saint.
Ephesians 1:5	I have been adopted as God's child.
Ephesians 2:18	I have direct access to God through the Holy Spirit.
Colossians 1:14	I have been redeemed and forgiven of all my sins.
Colossians 2:10	I am complete in Christ.

I AM SECURE:

Romans 8:1,2	I am free forever from condemnation.
Romans 8:28	I am assured that all things work together for good.
Romans 8:31f	If I am free from any condemning charges against me.
Romans 8:35f	If I cannot be separated from the love of God.
2 Corinthians 1:21,22	I have been established, anointed, and sealed by God.
Colossians 3:3	I am hidden with Christ in God.
Philippians 1:6	I am confident that the good work that God has begun in me will be perfected.
Philippians 3:20	I am a citizen of heaven.
2 Timothy 1:7	I have not been given a spirit of fear but of power, love, and a sound mind.
Hebrews 4:16	I can find grace and mercy in time of need.
1 John 5:18	I am born of God, and the evil one cannot touch me.

I AM SIGNIFICANT

Matthew 5:13,14	I am the salt and light of the earth.
John 15:1,5	I am a branch of the true vine, a channel of His life.
John 15:16	I have been chosen and appointed to bear fruit.
Acts 1:8	I am a personal witness of Christ's.
1 Corinthians 3:16	I am God's temple.
2 Corinthians 5:17f	I am a minister of reconciliation for God.
2 Corinthians 6:1	I am God's coworker (1 Corinthians 3:9).
Ephesians 2:6	I am seated with Christ in the heavenly realm.
Ephesians 2:10	I am God's workmanship.

| Ephesians 3:12 | I may approach God with freedom and confidence. |
| Philippians 4:13 | I can do all things through Christ who strengthens me. |